Microbiology and Biotechnology

Pauline Lowrie

Susan Wells

Series editor: Mary Jones

CAMBRIDGE
UNIVERSITY PRESS

PUBLISHED BY THE PRESS SYNDICATE OF THE UNIVERSITY OF CAMBRIDGE

The Pitt Building, Trumpington Street, Cambridge, United Kingdom

CAMBRIDGE UNIVERSITY PRESS

The Edinburgh Building, Cambridge CB2 2RU, UK

40 West 20th Street, New York, NY 10011–4211, USA

477 Williamstown Road, Port Melbourne, VIC 3207, Australia

Ruiz de Alarcón 13, 28014 Madrid, Spain

Dock House, The Waterfront, Cape Town 8001, South Africa

http://www.cambridge.org

© Cambridge University Press 2000

First published 2000
Third printing 2002

Printed in the United Kingdom
at the University Press, Cambridge

Typeface Swift   *System* QuarkXPress®

*A catalogue record for this book
is available from the British Library*

ISBN 0 521 78723 8 paperback

Produced by Gecko Ltd, Bicester, Oxon

Front cover photographs: Microbiologist with
petri dish/Matt Meadows, Peter Arnold Inc./
Science Photo Library

Acknowledgements

Photographs

1.1a, 1.21, NIBSC/Science Photo Library; 1.1b, Barry
Dowsett/Science Photo Library; 1.1c, CNRI/Science Photo
Library; 1.6, Dr L Caro/Science Photo Library; 1.17a,
Manfred Kage/Science Photo Library; 1.17b, 1.24,
Biophoto Associates; 1.17c, Dr Jeremy Burgess/Science
Photo Library; 1.17d, David Scharff/Science Photo
Library; 2.1, Peter Gould; 2.14, Crighton Thomas
Creative Limited; 3.1, James Holmes/Celltech Ltd/
Science Photo Library; 3.2, Geoff Tomkinson/Science
Photo Library; 3.4, Philippe Plailly/Science Photo
Library; 3.8, courtesy of Wearne Associates Ltd; 4.4,
Ronald Sheridan/Ancient Art & Architecture Collection
Ltd; 4.5, courtesy Ecosyl Products Limited; 5.4, Secchi-
Lecaque Roussel Uclaf/CNRI/Science Photo Library; 6.6,
Martin Bond/Science Photo Library; 6.7, Jerome
Yeats/Science Photo Library; 6.9, Sean Sprague/Panos
Pictures

Picture research: Maureen Cowdroy

The authors would also like to thank June Withenshaw
for her help with the 'newspaper article' on page 70,
and the publisher's team of editors and proofreaders
for all their work in the production of this new edition.

Contents

Introduction

Cambridge Advanced Sciences

The *Cambridge Advanced Sciences* series has been developed to meet the demands of all the new AS and A level science examinations. In particular, it has been endorsed by OCR as providing complete coverage of their specifications. The AS material is presented as a single text for each of biology, chemistry and physics. Material for the A2 year comprises six books in each subject: one of core material and one for each option. Some material has been drawn from the existing *Cambridge Modular Sciences* books; however, the majority is entirely new.

During the development of this series, the opportunity has been taken to improve the design, and a complete and thorough new writing and editing process has been applied. Much more material is now presented in colour. Although the existing *Cambridge Modular Sciences* texts do cover some of the new specifications, the *Cambridge Advanced Sciences* books cover every OCR learning objective in detail. They are the key to success in the new AS and A level examinations.

OCR is one of the three unitary awarding bodies offering the full range of academic and vocational qualifications in the UK. For full details of the new specifications, please contact OCR:

OCR, 1 Hills Road, Cambridge CB1 2EU
Tel: 01223 553311

The presentation of units

You will find that the books in this series use a bracketed convention in the presentation of units within tables and on graph axes. For example, ionisation energies of $1000\,kJ\,mol^{-1}$ and $2000\,kJ\,mol^{-1}$ will be represented in this way:

Measurement	Ionisation energy $(kJ\,mol^{-1})$
1	1000
2	2000

OCR examination papers use the solidus as a convention, thus:

Measurement	Ionisation energy / $kJ\,mol^{-1}$
1	1000
2	2000

Any numbers appearing in brackets with the units, for example $(10^{-5}\,mol\,dm^{-3}\,s^{-1})$, should be treated in exactly the same way as when preceded by the solidus, $/10^{-5}\,mol\,dm^{-3}\,s^{-1}$.

Microbiology and Biotechnology – an A2 option text

Microbiology and Biotechnology contains everything needed to cover the A2 option of the same name. It combines entirely new text and illustrations with revised and updated material from the first edition, previously available in the *Cambridge Modular Sciences* series.

The book is divided into six chapters corresponding to the components Microbiology, Techniques used in Microbiology and Cell Culture, Large-Scale Production, Biotechnology in Food Production, Biotechnology in Medicine, and Biotechnology in Industry and Public Health.

This second edition includes new material on plant cell and tissue culture in chapter 2, penicillin and mycoprotein production in chapter 3 and cheese production in chapter 4. The latter also includes discussion of the latest developments in genetic modification of plants and animals. This is continued in chapter 5 with mention of research into foods that deliver vaccines, and animal organ donation to humans, detailing both technical and ethical considerations. Chapter 6 now includes an expanded section on sewage processing methods as practised in the developed and developing worlds.

Terminology, classification and other data have all been updated throughout the book, to ensure accuracy and clarity. For the first time, a comprehensive glossary of terms is provided, linked via the index to the main content.

CHAPTER 1

Microbiology

By the end of this chapter you should be able to:

1 describe the distinguishing features of Prokaryotae, Protoctista, Fungi and viruses;

2 describe the general structure of viruses;

3 describe the life cycles of the lysogenic bacteriophage λ, and the Human Immunodeficiency Virus (HIV);

4 describe the organisation of the genetic material inside bacterial cells and viruses;

5 describe the structure and asexual reproduction of *Escherichia coli*;

6 describe the differences in bacterial cell wall structure that are the basis of the Gram staining technique.

The main purpose of this book is to give you an understanding of some of the many ways in which microbiology and biotechnology affect our lives. It is also important that you should understand why microorganisms are particularly suitable for use in industrial processes. However, before you can properly understand all these things, it is necessary that you learn a little about the structure and function of the different kinds of microorganisms.

Microorganisms (microbes) are so small that they can only be seen individually with a good quality light microscope. **Microbiology** is the study of microorganisms and can be sub-divided into several specialist branches such as **bacteriology** (the study of bacteria), **mycology** (the study of fungi) and **virology** (the study of viruses). There are four major groups of microorganisms: Prokaryotae, Protoctista, Fungi and viruses.

All prokaryotic organisms are grouped into the kingdom Prokaryotae. Prokaryotic cells do not have a true, membrane-bound nucleus and organelles, nor flagella with the typical 9+2 arrangement of microtubules such as are found in the eukaryotes (see *Biology 1* in this series). Organisms in the kingdoms Fungi and Protoctista are all eukaryotic. Viruses do not fit into a

classification of living organisms because they are dependent on other cells for their reproduction.

Kingdom Prokaryotae

This kingdom contains all the prokaryotic organisms, that is the bacteria and cyanobacteria (the blue-green bacteria, formerly called blue-green algae).

Bacteria

Examples: *Escherichia coli*, *Streptococcus lactis*, *Bacillus subtilis*, *Staphylococcus aureus*

Bacteria are found in a wide range of habitats: in soil, air, water, as well as in or on the surface of animals and plants. They range in size from 0.1–10 µm in length and are usually found in enormous numbers: one gram of soil may contain 100 million bacteria. Some bacteria have an optimum temperature for growth which is greater than 45 °C and are called thermophilic bacteria; some can even thrive in hot volcanic springs at around 70 °C. Psychrophilic bacteria, on the other hand, grow best at temperatures below 20 °C and can withstand long periods of freezing. Bacteria are important because they help to decay and recycle organic waste. Some cause disease, but most are harmless and many are of increasing economic importance in biotechnology.

Structure of bacteria

Figure 1.1 shows a variety of shapes of bacteria and *figure 1.2* shows the structure of a generalised bacterial cell. *Table 1.1* gives more details of their structure. Bacteria have no nucleus. Instead, they have a circular piece of double-stranded DNA which is often referred to as the bacterial chromosome. It is different from eukaryotic DNA because it is naked, i.e. it is not complexed with protein.

SAQ 1.1

Give two features present in the generalised bacterium which are not present in *E. coli*.

The bacterial cell wall

In 1884 Christian Gram developed a way of staining bacteria which divided them into two groups. These were called Gram-positive and Gram-negative. It is now known that bacteria have two different types of cell wall which the staining technique reveals.

The technique developed by Gram is still commonly used today. It involves heat-fixing a smear of bacteria to a clean microscope slide and then flooding it with crystal violet. All bacteria take up this stain. The smear is washed with Gram's iodine to fix the stain and then decolourised with alcohol or propanone. Gram-positive bacteria retain the crystal violet/iodine complex appearing purple, but Gram-negative bacteria do not. Finally the smear is counter-stained with a red stain such as safranin or carbol fuchsin. Gram-negative bacteria take up this stain and become red. Gram-positive bacteria stay purple.

The different reaction to the stain is due to the structure of the two basic types of cell wall (*figure 1.3*). Gram-positive bacteria have a plasma membrane surrounded by a rigid cell wall about 20–80 nm thick. This rigid layer is made of a peptidoglycan, (a polymer of sugars and amino acids) **murein**, which has a complex three-dimensional structure. Gram-negative bacteria also have a rigid layer outside the surface membrane but it is much thinner, only 2–3 nm thick. On the outside of this is an outer membrane which contains lipopolysaccharides instead of phospholipids. This

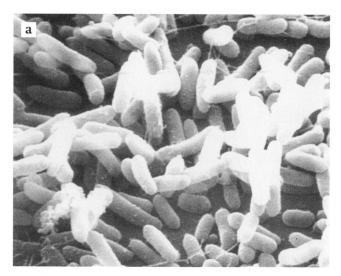

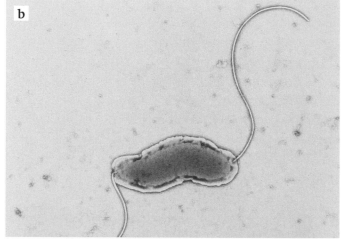

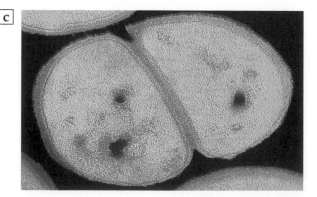

● **Figure 1.1** Some examples of bacteria.
a Scanning electron micrograph (SEM) of the rod-shaped Gram-negative bacterium *Escherichia coli* (× 14 500).
b Transmission EM of *Campylobacter jejunii* which causes food poisoning in humans. The bacterium moves by means of two single terminal flagella (× 9000).
c Transmission EM of *Staphylococcus aureus*. The cell has just divided (× 62 000).

Structure	Features
†cell wall	10–100 nm thick, net-like, multilayered structure made of peptidoglycans (polymers of sugars and amino acids); two distinct types are distinguished by the Gram's stain: **Gram-positive**; thicker, rigid murein network filled with peptides and polysaccharides, e.g. *Lactobacillus* **Gram-negative**: thinner, more complex, made of murein coated with a smooth layer of lipids, e.g. *E. coli*
†plasma membrane	phospholipid bilayer with proteins floating in membrane; proteins include enzymes involved in respiration†, photosynthesis•, nucleic acid synthesis† and electron transport†
†ribosomes	small 70S ribosomes are the site of protein synthesis
†cytoplasm	uniform with few organelles; contains storage granules, ribosomes, plasmids; a nuclear region is usually present
•plasmid	a small circular piece of DNA which is present in some bacteria, containing genes additional to those in the chromosome; some bacteria contain more than one
•flagellum	used in the locomotion of many motile bacteria; a rigid, hollow cylinder of protein, the base of which rotates propelling the cell along, e.g. *Rhizobium*, *Campylobacter* and *Azotobacter*
•capsule (slime layer)	an outer protective layer visible with negative (background) staining; it protects against chemicals and desiccation, stores waste products and protects the bacterium from attack by phagocytic cells; it helps bacteria to form colonies and is important in soil bacteria where it helps bind soil particles into crumbs, e.g. *Azotobacter*
•photosynthetic membranes	sac-like or tubular infoldings of the plasma membrane provide a large surface area for the inclusion of bacteriochlorophyll and other photosynthetic pigments in photoautotrophic bacteria, e.g. *Chromatium*
•mesosomes	tightly folded infoldings of the plasma membrane, that may be the site of respiration and involved in cell division and the uptake of DNA; they might be an artifact of preparation for electron microscopy
•pili (fimbriae)	numerous projections from the plasma membrane through the cell wall found all over some bacterial cells; they are used in conjugation to bind cells together and exchange genetic material; they also have an antigenic effect, e.g. *Salmonella*
•endospores	a hard outer covering forms a resistant endospore which ensures survival in severe conditions of drought, toxic chemicals and extremes of temperature, e.g. *Bacillus anthracis* spores, which cause the disease anthrax, are known to be viable after 50 years in the soil

†always present, •sometimes present

● **Table 1.1** Summary of the structure of bacteria.

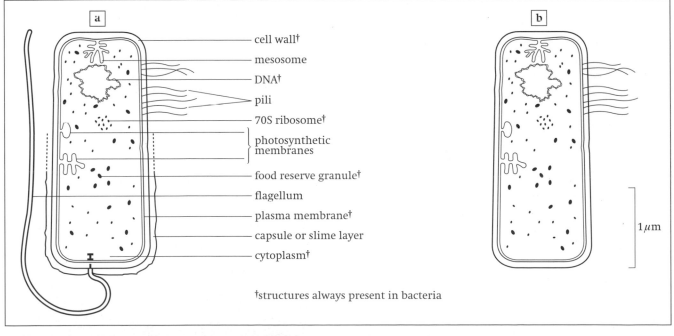

†structures always present in bacteria

● **Figure 1.2** **a** A generalised rod-shaped bacterial cell. **b** *Escherichia coli*.

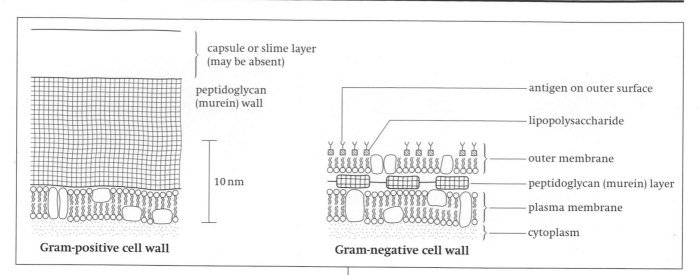

● Figure 1.3 The structure of bacterial cell walls based on electron micrographs of the cell walls of *Bacillus* (Gram-positive) and *E. coli* (Gram-negative).

forms an extra physical barrier to substances, such as antibiotics and enzymes like lysozyme, which normally destroy or inhibit bacteria. The crystal violet/iodine complex is a large molecule and it is thought that, during Gram staining, it becomes trapped inside the Gram-positive cell wall, whereas it is more easily washed out of the thinner Gram-negative cell wall.

Shapes of bacteria

When viewed with a microscope, bacteria show several distinct shapes and these may be used to help in identification (*figure 1.4*).

Reproduction

Bacteria grow very quickly in favourable conditions. The generation time may be as little as 20 minutes, though for many species it is 15–20 hours. Division is usually by binary fission (*figure 1.5*).

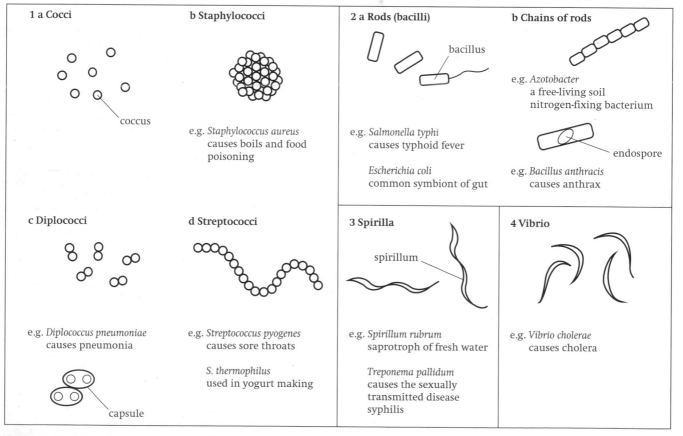

● Figure 1.4 The forms (shapes) of bacteria.

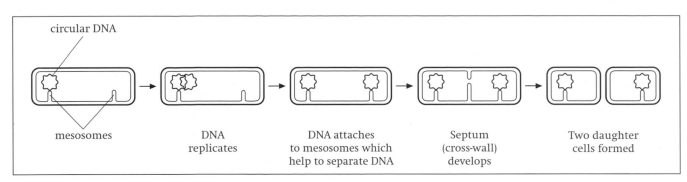

● **Figure 1.5** Binary fission in *Escherichia coli*.

The diagram labels, left to right: circular DNA; mesosomes; DNA replicates; DNA attaches to mesosomes which help to separate DNA; Septum (cross-wall) develops; Two daughter cells formed

1 The circular bacterial chromosome divides but there is no mitotic spindle. The chromosome attaches itself to the plasma membrane or, in some cases, to the mesosome.
2 A septum starts to be synthesised to divide the cell. This often starts growing where there are mesosomes.
3 The septum grows right across the cell, dividing it into two daughter cells.

Plasmids

The cytoplasm of certain bacteria contains one or more small circles of DNA called plasmids which are able to replicate independently of the main circular chromosome. Plasmids are known to carry genes which may help the bacterium to survive in adverse conditions. For example, plasmids known as R-factors cause resistance to antibiotics, virus infection and ultraviolet radiation. Plasmids can be transferred to another bacterium in conjugation, transformation or transduction.

Conjugation, transformation and transduction

Some bacteria have 'mating' cells which come together and are joined by their pili in a process known as **conjugation** (*figure 1.6*). The donor passes a plasmid called the F-factor, or fertility factor, to the recipient. Genetic information on the F-factor provides the bacterial cell with everything needed to be a donor, including the capacity to synthesise the sex pilus. The F-factor may exist as a free element within the cytoplasm, replicating independently of the bacterial chromosome, or it may become incorporated within the bacterial chromosome and be replicated whenever the chromosome replicates.

Transformation occurs when one bacterium releases DNA which is absorbed by a second bacterium. The second cell therefore acquires new characteristics.

Transduction is where new genes are inserted into the chromosome of a bacterium by a bacteriophage virus (see page 17).

Conjugation, transformation and transduction are not forms of sexual reproduction since fertilisation does not occur. In each of the above cases, DNA has been transferred from a donor to a recipient.

The economic importance of bacteria

Some genera of bacteria contain species which are commercially useful and some which are harmful to humans. For example, most *Bacillus* spp. live in

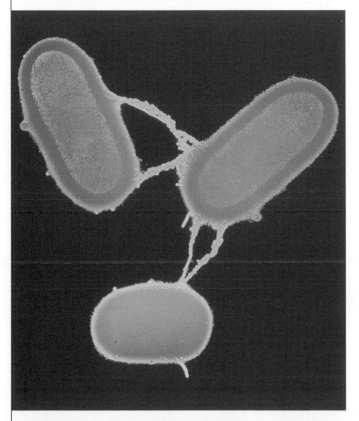

● **Figure 1.6** Conjugation in *E. coli*.

the soil, and are either aerobes or facultative anaerobes (see pages 34–35). *Bacillus subtilis* is a strict aerobe which is used in industry as a source of enzymes such as amylases. *Bacillus thuringiensis* has become important in genetic engineering because it causes a paralytic disease in many cater-pillars and has been used to produce insect-resistant plants (page 56). However, some species of *Bacillus* are pathogenic, such as *Bacillus anthracis* which causes the disease anthrax.

Table 1.2 lists some bacteria which are commercially useful. Some of these are described in more detail in later chapters. Other bacteria are useful in different ways, for example in recycling nutrients and fixing nitrogen in ecological cycles. As discussed in *Biology 1*, chapter 7, *Rhizobium* is a nitrogen-fixing bacterium which is present in the soil. It invades the root hairs of leguminous plants, causing the cells to divide and form nitrogen-fixing nodules. Many species of *Clostridium* can also fix nitrogen, such as *C. welchii*, *C. pastorianum* and *C. butylicum*, and are important in the nitrogen cycle. (Also see page 7.)

Table 1.3 lists some bacteria which cause disease in humans. Some belong to genera which contain many non-pathogenic species, for example most species of *Staphylococcus* are facultative anaerobes which are found in the normal microflora of the skin. *S. aureus* normally causes boils. However, one strain of this species (called MRSA, methicillin resistant *Staphylococcus aureus*) has developed resistance to most

Name	Gram stain	Form (shape)	Use
Lactobacillus bulgaricus	+ve	rods	yogurt
Streptococcus thermophilus	+ve	filamentous	yogurt
Streptococcus lactus	+ve	cocci	cheese
Streptococcus cremoris	+ve	cocci	cheese
Methylophilus methylotropus	variable	cocci	methane, methanol
Clostridium acetobutylicum	+ve	rods	propanone (acetone) and butanol
Leuconostoc mesenteroides	+ve	cocci	dextran
*Bacillus subtilis**	+ve	rods	enzymes
Streptomyces spp.	+ve	filamentous	antibiotics
*Escherichia coli**	–ve	rods	insulin, growth hormone, interferon
Pseudomonas denitrificans	–ve	rods	vitamin B_{12}

* using genetic engineering

● **Table 1.2** Some useful bacteria.

Name	Gram stain	Form (shape)	Disease
Staphylococcus aureus	+ve	cocci	boils
Salmonella typhimurium	–ve	rods	food poisoning
Salmonella typhi	–ve	rods	typhoid fever
Mycobacterium tuberculosis	variable	fine rods	tuberculosis
Bordetella pertussis	–ve	very short rods	whooping cough
Neisseria gonorrhoea	–ve	cocci	gonorrhoea
Treponema pallidum	variable	long spirals	syphilis
Vibrio cholerae	–ve	curved rods	cholera
Clostridium tetani	+ve	rods	tetanus
Clostridium botulinum	+ve	rods	botulism
Corynebacterium diphtheriae	+ve	short rods	diphtheria
Listeria spp.	+ve	round-ended rods	listeriosis
Shigella sonnei	–ve	rods	dysentery
Yersinia pestis	–ve	small rods	plague

● **Table 1.3** Some harmful bacteria.

antibiotics, through their overuse, and has become a major problem in hospitals in many countries. MRSA can cause severe blood-poisoning (septicaemia) when it infects wounds, e.g. after sugery. This is difficult to treat and can be fatal.

SAQ 1.2

Match the words on the left to the definitions on the right.

plasmid — slimy layer surrounding some bacterial cell walls

mesosome — circular piece of DNA not joined to chromosome

cell wall — made of pilin, used in conjugation in some species

capsule — the main component of this is the peptidoglycan murein

pilus — infolding of membrane, probably used in cell division

Cyanobacteria (blue-green bacteria)

Examples: *Anabaena cylindrica*, *Nostoc muscorum*, *Spirulina platensis*

Cyanobacteria are prokaryotic microorganisms similar to the true bacteria. They are photo-synthetic but are not true algae because they do not have membrane-bound nuclei, and are considered to be very ancient life-forms. They have been found in fossil remains from over three billion years ago and may have been some of the first living organisms to evolve on Earth. They are found in the surface layer of fresh and sea water. On land they will grow wherever there is both light and moisture and are found as slime on the surface of mud, rocks, wood and on some living organisms, such as the sloth. Their name comes from the photosynthetic pigments which give them a distinct dark greenish-blue colour.

Structure of cyanobacteria

Blue-greens have a typical prokaryotic cell structure since they have a naked coil of DNA and no true nucleus (*figure 1.7*). The cell wall is similar in structure and composition to that of Gram-negative bacteria. Protein synthesis takes place on 70S ribosomes in the cytoplasm. Blue-greens are photosynthetic. They have chlorophyll and carotenoid pigments incorporated into infoldings of the plasma membrane, called **lamellae**. They also have photosynthetic pigments, such as phycocyanin and phycoerythrin, which are present in phycobilisomes. These give the cells their distinctive colouration. The cells may occur singly or in colonies, but members of a colony remain independent.

Nitrogen fixation

Only a very few organisms are capable of fixing atmospheric nitrogen by reducing it to ammonia and combining it with organic acids to produce amino acids and proteins. Nitrogen-fixing bacteria can do this and so can some blue-greens. Cells able to fix nitrogen contain the enzyme nitrogen-ase. This enzyme is inactivated by oxygen and so conditions inside the nitrogen-fixing cell have to be anaerobic. Some blue-greens, such as *Anabaena*, have special thick-walled cells called **heterocysts**.

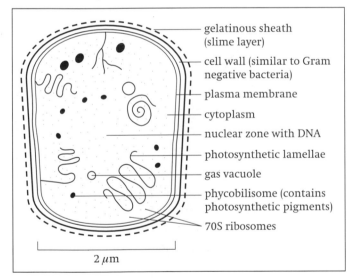

gelatinous sheath (slime layer)

cell wall (similar to Gram negative bacteria)

plasma membrane

cytoplasm

nuclear zone with DNA

photosynthetic lamellae

gas vacuole

phycobilisome (contains photosynthetic pigments)

70S ribosomes

2 μm

● **Figure 1.7** Diagram of a typical blue-green cell (based on electron micrographs).

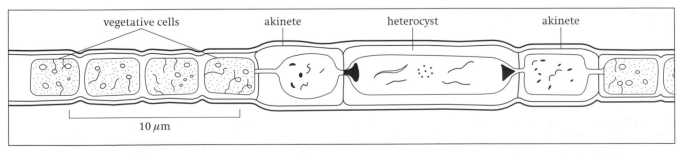

vegetative cells   akinete   heterocyst   akinete

10 μm

● **Figure 1.8** A filament of *Anabaena*.

Anabaena has filaments made up of many normal photosynthetic cells that produce sugars and oxygen. Scattered along the filaments are a few distinct heterocyst cells that are able to fix atmospheric nitrogen in this way (*figure 1.8*).

Many filamentous blue-greens are also able to produce **akinetes**, or spores. These are able to survive adverse conditions, such as a period of overpopulation known as an algal 'bloom', and seem to develop from a vegetative cell near to a heterocyst. The cell increases in size and accumulates large food reserves. Photosynthesis within the akinete is reduced and gas vacuoles disappear. This means that the akinete slowly sinks to the bottom of the water. It may survive for several years, and will germinate as soon as conditions become favourable.

The economic importance of blue-greens

Spirulina platensis is a filamentous blue-green found naturally in shallow alkaline lakes in parts of Africa and South America. For thousands of years it has been collected and dried by the local people and used as a food. It is often fried or put in soups and sauces; it is also used as cattle food. *Nostoc* is another blue-green which is used as a food in Peru and in South-East Asia.

In agriculture, nitrogen-fixing blue-greens may be used as organic fertilisers. They are grown on a large scale in China, India, Indonesia and the Philippines, particularly where rice is cultivated in paddy fields. The water may be seeded with a starter culture of blue-greens at the beginning of the growing season. This method has been shown to increase the yield of rice by 15–20%.

Research is taking place into the use of blue-greens in a solar energy conversion system. As you have just learnt, *Anabaena cylindrica* has heterocysts to fix nitrogen and is also able to give off oxygen by photosynthesis in the vegetative cells. In the absence of atmospheric nitrogen it gives off hydrogen by nitrogenase-catalysed electron transfer to H^+ ions in the heterocysts. Both oxygen and hydrogen are in demand industrially.

SAQ 1.3

Why are blue-greens classified as prokaryotes?

SAQ 1.4

It is thought that blue-greens may have been the first photosynthetic organisms on Earth and that they represent a very early stage in the evolution of life. Give as many reasons as you can why this might be so.

Kingdom Protoctista

This kingdom has been created to contain all groups of eukaryotic organisms which are neither animals, plants, fungi nor prokaryotes. These groups are not really related though they do have some similarities. They include all protozoa, all nucleated algae and the slime moulds (*figure 1.9* and *table 1.4*).

The **protozoa** is a collective term for the phyla Rhizopoda, Zoomastigina, Apicomplexa and Ciliophora. They are found wherever moisture is present, in sea water, fresh water and soil. There are commensal, symbiotic and parasitic species in addition to many free-living types. Protozoa are eukaryotic. The nucleus has a **nuclear envelope**, and movement is by means of a variety of locomotory structures such as flagella, cilia or **pseudopodia**. Since the cytoplasm of freshwater protozoans is usually hypertonic to (more concentrated than) the aqueous environment, they take in water by osmosis. To counteract this, they have **contractile vacuoles** that act as pumps to remove excess water from the cytoplasm. However, contractile vacuoles may also be found in some marine protozoans. All types of nutrition are found in protozoans: some are autotrophic, others are saprotrophic and many are heterotrophic. Digestion of food takes place in **food vacuoles** in the cytoplasm. Gas exchange is by diffusion across the plasma membrane. Waste products from cell metabolism diffuse out of the cell. The main nitrogenous waste is ammonia.

The economic importance of protozoa

Many ciliates are saprotrophs and are vital in the recycling of organic wastes, particularly in sewage treatment. Parasitic forms, such as *Entamoeba*, which causes amoebic dysentery, and *Plasmodium*, which causes malaria, may cause loss of life.

Malaria, for example, can be devastating to the economy of developing countries, incapacitating millions of workers every year (*Biology 1*, chapter 15).

SAQ 1.5 _____
List three features shared by the four phyla classed as protozoa, and two features which distinguish them from each other.

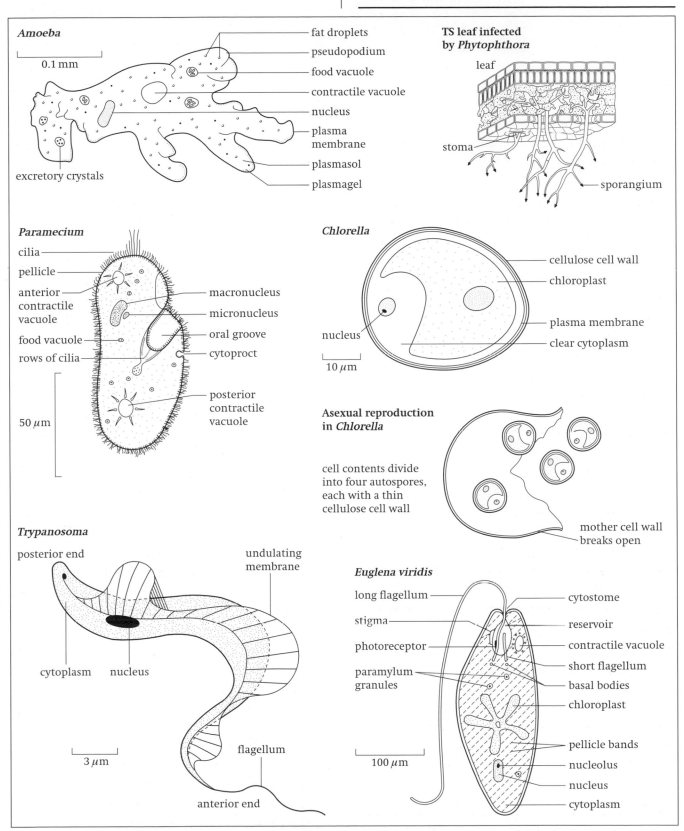

● **Figure 1.9** The structure of some representative protoctists.

Phylum	Example	Structure	Locomotion	Nutrition	Reproduction	Importance
Rhizopoda	*Amoeba proteus*	0.5 mm long, single cell, cytoplasm exists in two states: plasmasol and plasmagel	pseudopodia	phagocytosis and food vacuoles formed	asexual by binary fission	*Entamoeba histolytica* causes amoebic dysentery
Apicomplexa (sporozoans)	*Plasmodium vivax*	10 μm long, different forms during life cycle: sporozoites long and thin, infective particles; merozoites smaller, pear-shaped	microtubules which slide over each other to penetrate host tissue	phagocytosis	asexual by multiple fission and sexual by gametocytes	*P. vivax* causes parasitic disease malaria, mosquito is the vector
Ciliophora (ciliates)	*Paramecium caudatum*	100 μm long, enclosed by a pellicle with cilia, oral groove leads to 'mouth' with cytostome	cilia beat together in coordinated way	cilia beat and sweep food towards cytostome, where phagocytosis takes place	asexual by binary fission, sexual by conjugation	live in fresh water, important in sewage treatment and decomposition
Zoomastigina (flagellates)	*Trypanosoma gambiense*	unicellular, elongated spindle-shaped.	single flagellum bound to the trypanosome along the length of the cell by the undulating membrane, free beyond that; wave-like movements propel the cell through the viscous blood plasma	heterotrophic, parasitic; lives in human blood plasma; soluble nutrients diffuse into cell	longitudinal binary fission in the blood of the host starting at anterior end	causes trypanosomiasis or 'sleeping sickness'; spread by the tsetse fly as it feeds on human blood; symptoms include headache, anaemia, inflammation of brain and spinal cord
Euglenophyta (euglenoid flagellates)	*Euglena viridis*	300 μm long slender cell, pellicle covers outside, blunt anterior end with reservoir	two flagella arise from base of reservoir, light-sensitive stigma used to orientate movement	chloroplasts present, therefore photoauto-trophic; stores food granules of paramylum, needs vitamins B_1 and B_{12} for growth	longitudinal binary fission (asexual)	found in fresh and salt water, and damp soil

● **Table 1.4** A summary of the Kingdom Protoctista (continued opposite).

Phylum	Example	Structure	Locomotion	Nutrition	Reproduction	Importance
Chlorophyta (green algae)	*Chlorella vulgaris*	50 µm diameter, unicellular green alga, thin cellulose cell wall, large cup-shaped chloroplast	floats in water	photoauto-trophic	asexual by fission (*figure 1.9*)	freshwater ponds
Oomycota (oomycetes)	*Phytophthora infestans* or *Pythium* spp.	long thread-like hyphae, aseptate (no cross walls), cytoplasm contains many nuclei, cell wall of chitin with mannan and glucan polymers	spore stages have two flagella	heterotrophic (plant parasites), hyphae secrete enzymes, food digested extra-cellularly, soluble nutrients absorbed	asexual by motile spores formed inside a sporangium on a special hypha (sporangiophore); sexual by fusion of male antheridium and female oogonium to produce sexual oospore which survives adverse conditions	*Phytophthora* causes late blight of potatoes (as in Irish potato famine) *Pythium* causes damping-off in seedlings
Myxomycota (slime moulds)	*Macbrideola synsporus*	a naked mass of protoplasm called the plasmodium, which moves along engulfing and digesting small particles, e.g. bacteria, yeasts and fungal spores	protoplasmic streaming: some spores amoeboid, some flagellated	heterotrophic	sexual by fusion of spores	widely distributed in damp environments

● **Table 1.4** (continued).

Kingdom Fungi

Fungi are obligate aerobes, which are killed in the absence of oxygen, or facultative anaerobes, which grow best when oxygen is available but are able to survive anaerobic conditions. They are found almost everywhere. They are eukaryotic organisms with a cell wall that is usually made of chitin. Fungi are not photosynthetic but heterotrophic, deriving their nutrients by absorption of organic materials.

Fungi are usually filamentous or thread-like. The individual threads are called **hyphae** which are usually multinucleate; these branch profusely, often fusing together to form a tangled mass of branched hyphae called the **mycelium**. Individual hyphae are surrounded by rigid cell walls and grow only at their tips. It is this form of **apical growth** that separates fungi from almost all other organisms, even filamentous ones.

Since fungi are eukaryotic, they have distinct nuclei each surrounded by a nuclear envelope with pores; they have chromosomes and a spindle that appears during nuclear division.

Mitochondria are found in the cytoplasm and there is extensive endoplasmic reticulum (ER) (*figure 1.10*); ribosomes are found both free in the cytoplasm and attached to the ER. These ribosomes are the larger (80S) type which is typical of eukaryotic cells. The cytoplasm also contains numerous vacuoles containing storage materials such as starch, lipid globules and volutin.

The cytoplasm and organelles are surrounded by a selectively permeable, phospholipid unit membrane (plasma membrane). The cytoplasm is at its most dense at the tips of the hyphae. The older parts of the mycelium are often metabolically inactive with large vacuoles in the cytoplasm. In septate species there are pores in the cross-walls to allow substances in solution, and also structures such as nuclei, to move freely from one section to another.

The growth of hyphae is very rapid under favourable conditions. Each hypha grows at the tip and branches repeatedly along its length to reach new food supplies and grow away from its own waste products (*figure 1.11*).

Phylum Zygomycota (zygomycetes)

Example: *Mucor hiemalis*

In zygomycetes the hyphae are non-septate and make a large, well-developed branching mycelium. Asexual reproduction is by non-motile spores formed in a **sporangium** borne on a **sporangiophore** (*figure 1.12*). Sexual reproduction is shown in *figure 1.13*.

Phylum Ascomycota (ascomycetes)

Examples: *Penicillium notatum, Saccharomyces cerevisiae, Aspergillus niger, Neurospora* spp.

All ascomycetes have septate hyphae. In asexual reproduction, non-motile spores, called **conidia**, are formed on special hyphal branches called conidiophores. Sexual reproduction is complex. The male gamete is in a structure called the **antheridium** and the female gamete is in a structure called the **ascogonium**. If the antheridium and ascogonium contact each other, the cell walls break down and the two nuclei fuse. A diploid **ascus** is formed. Meiosis occurs in the ascus, followed by mitosis, to release eight haploid **ascospores**. These act as resting cells and

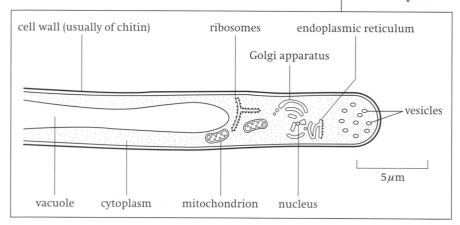

● **Figure 1.10** Diagram of the tip of a typical fungal hypha (based on electron micrographs).

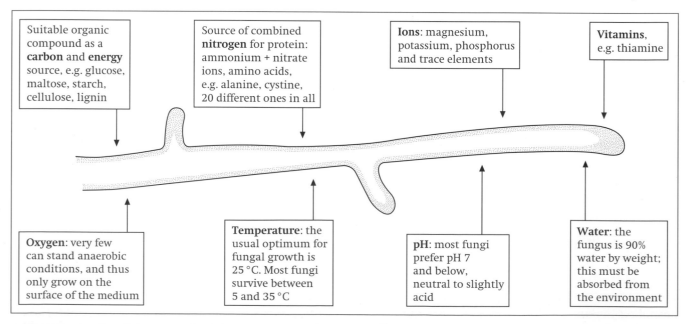

● **Figure 1.11** Conditions required for fungal growth.

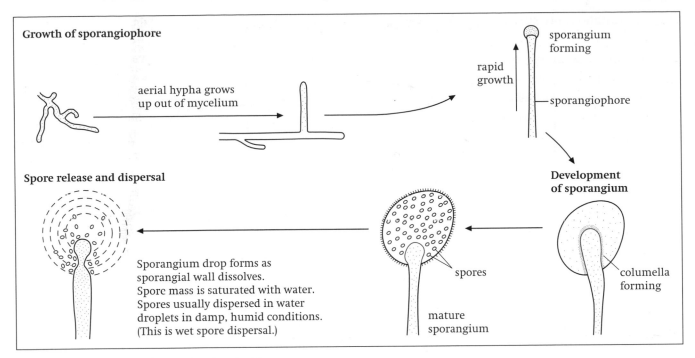

Growth of sporangiophore

aerial hypha grows up out of mycelium

rapid growth

sporangium forming

sporangiophore

Development of sporangium

columella forming

spores

mature sporangium

Spore release and dispersal

Sporangium drop forms as sporangial wall dissolves. Spore mass is saturated with water. Spores usually dispersed in water droplets in damp, humid conditions. (This is wet spore dispersal.)

● **Figure 1.12** Asexual reproduction in *Mucor*.

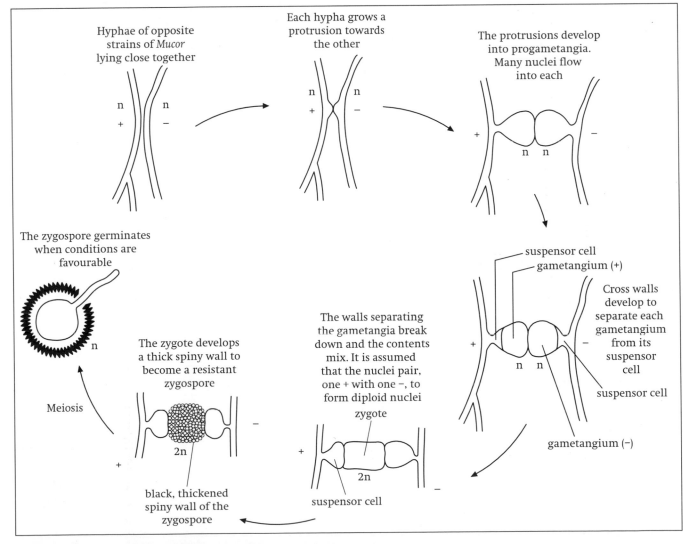

Hyphae of opposite strains of *Mucor* lying close together

Each hypha grows a protrusion towards the other

The protrusions develop into progametangia. Many nuclei flow into each

suspensor cell
gametangium (+)

Cross walls develop to separate each gametangium from its suspensor cell

suspensor cell

gametangium (−)

The walls separating the gametangia break down and the contents mix. It is assumed that the nuclei pair, one + with one −, to form diploid nuclei

zygote

suspensor cell

The zygote develops a thick spiny wall to become a resistant zygospore

black, thickened spiny wall of the zygospore

The zygospore germinates when conditions are favourable

Meiosis

● **Figure 1.13** Sexual reproduction in *Mucor*: conjugation.

later germinate to produce a new generation.

Yeasts, such as *Saccharomyces cerevisiae*, are unicellular ascomycetes and are industrially important fungi. They have been used for centuries in the making of bread, the brewing of beer and in winemaking. They are unicellular organisms, differing from other fungi in that the cell wall is composed largely of polymers of mannan and glucan (*figure 1.14*). Sexual reproduction in yeast cells is by fusion (*figure 1.15*).

Phylum Basidiomycota (basidiomycetes)

Examples: *Agaricus campestris*, *Puccinia graminis*

All basidiomycetes have septate hyphae. Asexual reproduction is usually absent. Sexual reproduction is usually by the fusion of vegetative hyphae from two mating types. The nuclei of the two hyphae do not fuse, and the fungus exists for most of its life as a **dikaryon**, with two types of nucleus in its hyphae (*figure 1.16*). Later a complex fruiting body is formed. This **basidiocarp** contains many **basidia** in which the nuclei fuse and meiosis takes place. Four haploid basidiospores are produced from each basidium to complete the life cycle.

The mushroom *Agaricus* is cultivated for food on a large scale. There are many other fungi which are nutritious and edible (*figure 1.17*) although some are notoriously poisonous.

Fungal spores

At some stage in all fungal life cycles, spores are produced on a

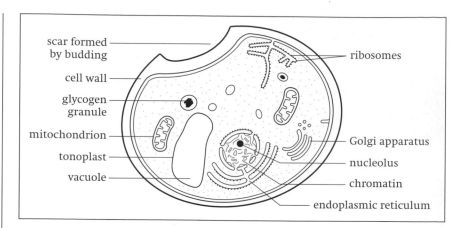

● **Figure 1.14** Section through *Saccharomyces* cell (based on electron micrographs ×10 000).

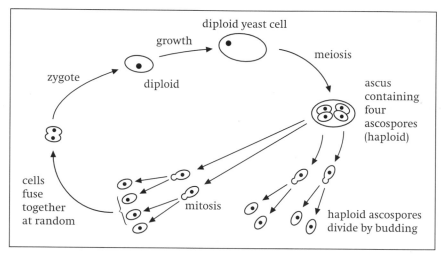

● **Figure 1.15** Sexual reproduction in the yeast *Saccharomyces cerevisiae*.

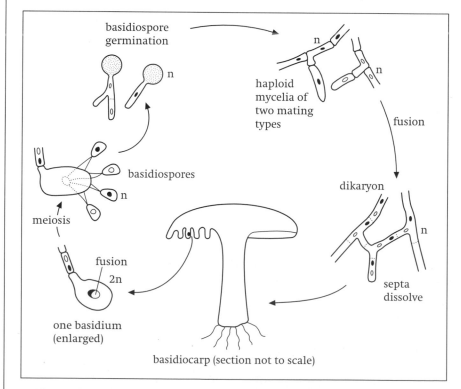

● **Figure 1.16** The life cycle of a generalised basidiomycete.

specialised part of the mycelium. The spores are dormant structures though many are short-lived. They have little resistance to desiccation, ultraviolet light or predators. Vast numbers of spores are produced and dispersed. If they do not land in favourable conditions and are not destroyed they remain dormant. In favourable conditions the spore quickly swells, a germ tube grows out and the hypha elongates rapidly and soon branches. This process is called **germination**.

The economic importance of fungi

Table 1.5 shows examples of useful and harmful fungi.

Some useful fungi	Use
Penicillium notatum	antibiotic penicillin
Penicillium chrysogenum	antibiotic penicillin
Penicillium griseofulvum	antibiotic griseofulvin
Penicillium roquefortii	cheese ripening
Penicillium camembertii	cheese ripening
Aspergillus fumigatus	antibiotic fumagillin (used against amoebic dysentery)
Aspergillus niger	citric acid production
Fusarium graminearum	mycoprotein production
Candida spp.	single-cell protein from waste hydrocarbons
Saccharomyces cerevisiae	brewing, baking, winemaking
Saccharomyces carlsbergensis	brewing
Agaricus campestris	food (edible mushroom)

Some harmful fungi	Host	Disease
Rhizopus stolonifer	fruit	soft rot
Erysiphe spp.	cereals	powdery mildew
Ceratocystis ulmi	elm	Dutch elm disease
Claviceps purpurea	rye	ergot (infected rye can be fatal if eaten due to toxic alkaloids produced by the fungus)
Puccinia graminis	wheat	rusts
Trichophyton spp.	humans	athlete's foot, ringworm
Candida utilis	humans	oral/vaginal thrush

● **Figure 1.17** Some examples of fungi.
a Scanning EM of *Saccharomyces cerevisiae* (brewers' yeast, ×8000).
b *Agaricus* sp. (edible mushrooms).
c *Penicillium chrysogenum*, a mould used to produce the antibiotic penicillin (×10).
d *Aspergillus niger*, showing conidiophores (×500).

● **Table 1.5** The economic importance of fungi.

SAQ 1.6

What are the main distinguishing features of:

a Ascomycota; **b** Basidiomycota; **c** Zygomycota?

SAQ 1.7

What features do fungi:

a have in common with higher plants,

b have different from higher plants?

SAQ 1.8

Explain the meaning of the following terms:
hypha; mycelium; septum; bud; basidium.

Viruses

Viruses have no cellular structure. They are all obligate parasites, which means they can only reproduce when inside other living cells. Outside cells, they show no metabolic activity or any sign of life, and are rather like complex crystals. They are about 50 times smaller than bacteria, ranging from 20 nm to about 300 nm and therefore cannot be seen with a light microscope. They were known to be infective agents, able to pass through filters which retained bacteria, as early as 1892. However, their structure was shown only by extensive studies using the electron microscope.

Structure of viruses

Viruses consist of a core containing genetic material of double-stranded or single-stranded DNA or RNA. This is surrounded by a protective coat of protein called a **capsid**, made up of sub-units called **capsomeres** (*figure 1.18*). Some viruses have an envelope of lipoprotein around the capsid.

Shapes of viruses

There are three basic viral shapes as shown in *table 1.6*. These are polyhedral, helical and complex.

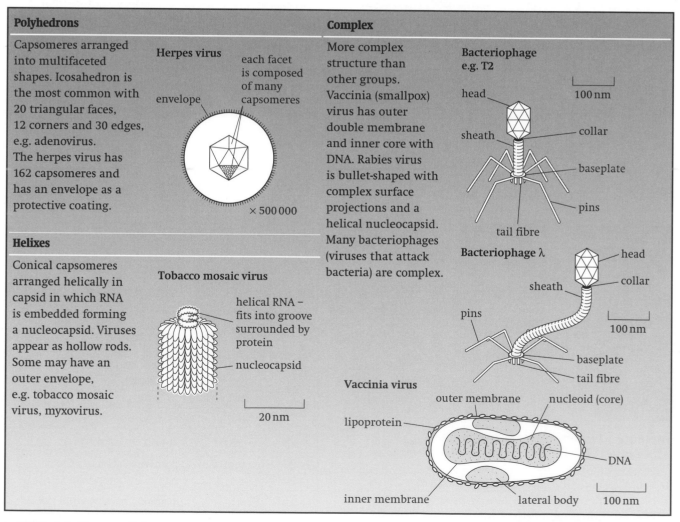

Polyhedrons		Complex	
Capsomeres arranged into multifaceted shapes. Icosahedron is the most common with 20 triangular faces, 12 corners and 30 edges, e.g. adenovirus. The herpes virus has 162 capsomeres and has an envelope as a protective coating.	**Herpes virus** — each facet is composed of many capsomeres — envelope — × 500 000	More complex structure than other groups. Vaccinia (smallpox) virus has outer double membrane and inner core with DNA. Rabies virus is bullet-shaped with complex surface projections and a helical nucleocapsid. Many bacteriophages (viruses that attack bacteria) are complex.	**Bacteriophage e.g. T2** — head — 100 nm — sheath — collar — baseplate — pins — tail fibre
Helixes			**Bacteriophage λ** — head — collar — sheath — pins — 100 nm — baseplate — tail fibre
Conical capsomeres arranged helically in capsid in which RNA is embedded forming a nucleocapsid. Viruses appear as hollow rods. Some may have an outer envelope, e.g. tobacco mosaic virus, myxovirus.	**Tobacco mosaic virus** — helical RNA – fits into groove surrounded by protein — nucleocapsid — 20 nm		**Vaccinia virus** — outer membrane — nucleoid (core) — lipoprotein — DNA — inner membrane — lateral body — 100 nm

● **Table 1.6** Shapes of viruses.

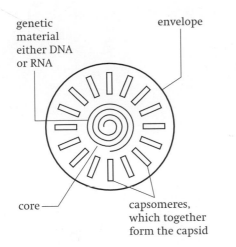

genetic material either DNA or RNA

envelope

core

capsomeres, which together form the capsid

● **Figure 1.18** A generalised virus.

The life cycle of a virus

The life cycle of a bacteriophage virus, such as T2, is shown in *figure 1.19*.

Bacteriophages are important industrially because they can be used as cloning vectors, to transfer pieces of DNA to bacterial cells (see chapter 4). They are also important because they infect and destroy their host bacteria. Bacteriophage infection can destroy a fermentation process involving bacteria and cause the loss of several days' production. The whole industrial plant may need to be closed down for thorough sterilisation.

Most viruses have a similar life cycle to a bacteriophage. However, they have different ways of penetrating animal and plant cells (*figure 1.20*) and are released differently too. A few viruses burst their host cell during release. Others leave the cell by a process similar to penetration in reverse. Enveloped viruses are released by budding, taking an envelope of the host cell membrane as they escape (*figure 1.21*).

Some viruses do not replicate once inside the host cell but instead their nucleic acid becomes incorporated into the DNA of the host cell. The virus is then known as a **provirus** since it is inactive, and the host cell is said to be **lysogenic** since it is capable of lysis once the virus becomes active (*figure 1.22*). This process is called **transduction**. In the lysogenic cycle, the host cell is not destroyed by the virus. One example of a lysogenic phage is lambda (λ) phage. This is a virus of *E. coli* that can be used in genetic engineering to insert new genes into its host.

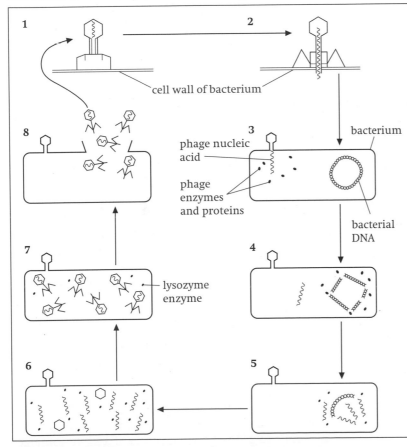

cell wall of bacterium

phage nucleic acid

phage enzymes and proteins

bacterium

bacterial DNA

lysozyme enzyme

1 Bacteriophage tail fibres adsorb onto specific receptor sites on bacterial cell wall.

2 Tail fibres bend and baseplate is anchored by pins to cell surface. Tail sheath contracts and hollow spike is pushed into cell aided by enzymes.

3 Nucleic acid is injected into bacterium with enzymes and viral proteins.

4 Phage enzymes break down bacterial DNA.

5 Phage DNA takes over control of the cell.

6 Phage DNA replicates and codes for new viral proteins.

7 New phages are assembled; lysozyme enzyme made by phage DNA.

8 Cell lysis (bursting) due to build-up of lysozyme. Phages released (up to 1000) to infect other bacteria.

Time for lytic cycle is approximately 30 minutes.

● **Figure 1.19** The lytic cycle of a bacteriophage virus.

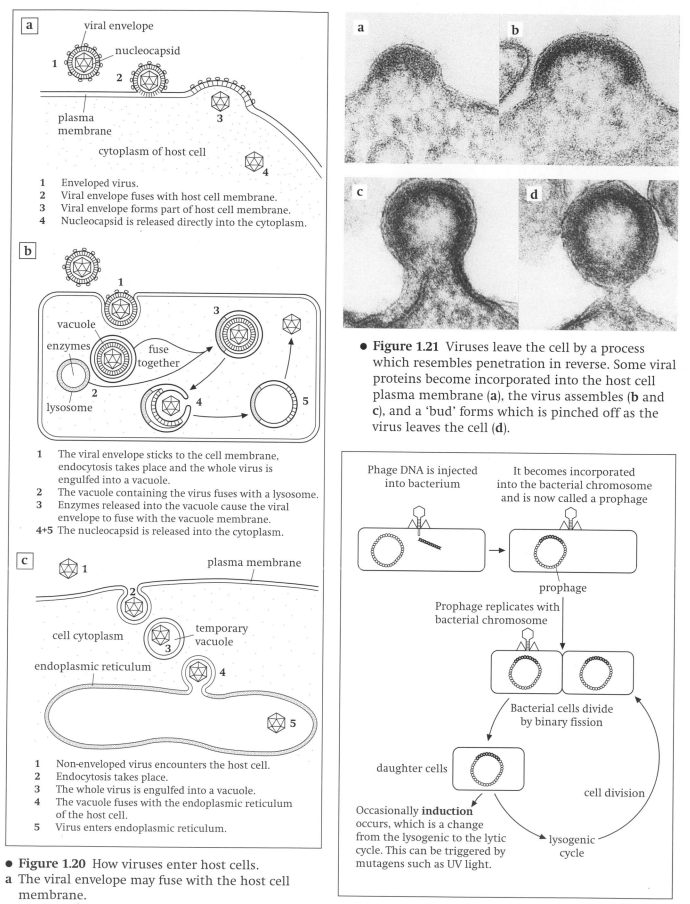

a

viral envelope
nucleocapsid
1
2
3
plasma membrane
cytoplasm of host cell
4

1 Enveloped virus.
2 Viral envelope fuses with host cell membrane.
3 Viral envelope forms part of host cell membrane.
4 Nucleocapsid is released directly into the cytoplasm.

b

1
vacuole
3
enzymes
fuse together
lysosome
2
4
5

1 The viral envelope sticks to the cell membrane, endocytosis takes place and the whole virus is engulfed into a vacuole.
2 The vacuole containing the virus fuses with a lysosome.
3 Enzymes released into the vacuole cause the viral envelope to fuse with the vacuole membrane.
4+5 The nucleocapsid is released into the cytoplasm.

c

1
plasma membrane
2
cell cytoplasm
3
temporary vacuole
endoplasmic reticulum
4
5

1 Non-enveloped virus encounters the host cell.
2 Endocytosis takes place.
3 The whole virus is engulfed into a vacuole.
4 The vacuole fuses with the endoplasmic reticulum of the host cell.
5 Virus enters endoplasmic reticulum.

● **Figure 1.20** How viruses enter host cells.
a The viral envelope may fuse with the host cell membrane.
b Endocytosis.
c How a non-enveloped virus enters a cell.

a   **b**

c   **d**

● **Figure 1.21** Viruses leave the cell by a process which resembles penetration in reverse. Some viral proteins become incorporated into the host cell plasma membrane (**a**), the virus assembles (**b** and **c**), and a 'bud' forms which is pinched off as the virus leaves the cell (**d**).

Phage DNA is injected into bacterium

It becomes incorporated into the bacterial chromosome and is now called a prophage

prophage

Prophage replicates with bacterial chromosome

Bacterial cells divide by binary fission

daughter cells

cell division

Occasionally **induction** occurs, which is a change from the lysogenic to the lytic cycle. This can be triggered by mutagens such as UV light.

lysogenic cycle

● **Figure 1.22** The lysogenic cycle of a bacteriophage virus, e.g. λ phage.

Viruses as disease-causing agents

Since viruses are always parasitic they usually cause some symptoms of disease in their host. They are of economic importance because of the loss of human and animal life caused by some types, or because infection by the many less virulent types (*table 1.7*) may prevent people being able to work. Plant viruses cause tremendous losses in cultivated crops particularly in areas of monoculture (*table 1.8*).

Virus	Structure	Genetic material	Disease
herpes simplex type 1	icosahedral, enveloped	double-stranded DNA	cold sores
type 2	icosahedral, enveloped	double-stranded DNA	genital herpes
varicella zoster	icosahedral, enveloped	double-stranded DNA	chickenpox
adenovirus	icosahedral, non-enveloped	double-stranded DNA	pharyngitis, conjunctivitis
variola major	complex	double-stranded DNA	smallpox
hepatitis B	icosahedral, enveloped	double-stranded DNA	serum hepatitis
parvovirus	icosahedral, non-enveloped	single-stranded DNA	viral gastroenteritis
polio virus	icosahedral, non-enveloped	single-stranded RNA	poliomyelitis
rhinovirus	icosahedral, non-enveloped	single-stranded RNA	common cold
rubella virus	icosahedral, enveloped	single-stranded RNA	German measles (rubella)
mumps virus	helical, enveloped	single-stranded RNA	mumps
influenza virus	helical, enveloped	single-stranded RNA	influenza
rabies virus	bullet-shaped helical, enveloped	single-stranded RNA	rabies
human immunodeficiency virus (HIV)	spherical, enveloped	single-stranded RNA	acquired immunodeficiency syndrome (AIDS)

● **Table 1.7** Some viruses that cause human disease.

Virus	Shape	Genetic material	Vector	Symptoms
tobacco mosaic, tomato mosaic, cucumber green-mottle	elongated	RNA	mechanical contact, grafts, fungus	yellow-brown mottled patches on leaves
cauliflower mosaic	spherical	DNA	aphids	yellow mottled leaves, poor growth
tobacco ringspot, tomato ringspot	spherical	RNA	seedborne, nematodes	ring-like patches, brown-white on leaves
barley yellows dwarf, soybean dwarf	spherical	RNA	aphids	stunted growth, yellow leaves
tomato spotted wilt	spherical enveloped	RNA	thrips	wilting leaves, discoloured spots on leaves
turnip yellow mosaic	spherical	RNA	beetle	yellow mottled patches on leaves
potato X virus, narcissus mosaic	elongated	RNA	mechanical contact or damage	mottled leaves, poor growth
tobacco rattle	elongated	RNA	nematodes	dry, brown papery leaves
beet yellows, wheat yellow leaf, beet yellow stunt	elongated	RNA	aphids	stunted growth, yellow leaves

● **Table 1.8** Some viruses that cause plant disease.

Retroviruses

Retroviruses are a group of viruses with two unusual features. Firstly, they have single-stranded RNA as their genetic material, instead of DNA. To infect cells they must carry the enzyme **reverse transcriptase** which converts the viral RNA into DNA once the virus starts to replicate inside the host cell.

Secondly, when the DNA copy of the viral genes is inserted into the host cell's chromosomes it forms a **provirus**. The viral infection can stay latent for some time, even several years, before the provirus is expressed to make new RNA and further virus particles. However, during this latent period, every time the host cell divides the provirus is replicated too, so that the number of infected cells increases.

SAQ 1.9 _____

Compare the lytic and lysogenic cycles.

SAQ 1.10 _____

Do you consider viruses to be alive? Give reasons to justify your answer.

Various retroviruses have been discovered in animals and humans, but the most well known is human immunodeficiency virus (HIV) which causes AIDS (acquired immunodeficiency syndrome). HIV infects T helper lymphocytes and macrophages and destroys them. A very unusual feature of AIDS is that there is considerable variation between viruses isolated from different people, with no two viruses appearing to be exactly the same. As we saw in *Biology 1*, chapter 15, HIV is spread in three main ways:

- by sexual contact with an infected person;
- by an infected woman passing it on to her baby through the placenta;
- by blood from an infected person entering another person's bloodstream, either through sharing needles, receiving infected blood during transfusion or through a wound.

HIV follows a similar pattern of infection to other retroviruses (*figure 1.23*). While in the provirus state, it is largely hidden from the immune system. This stage can last from two to ten years, during which time the person appears healthy and feels well. After this dormant phase, the number of T cells in the body falls dramatically as infected T cells are destroyed. This marks the beginning of AIDS. The infected person's immunodeficiency means they frequently become infected by other bacteria and viruses, leading to diseases, such as pneumonia, which may result in death.

Researchers are trying to develop drugs against AIDS. Zydovudine, or AZT, prevents reverse transcriptase making DNA from RNA, while other drugs block the receptor on the host cell, preventing the virus entering the cell. Another approach is the use of recombinant DNA technology and genetic engineering to make copies of the host cell's receptor proteins. These bind to the outer coat of the virus and prevent it attaching to cells. However, these drugs do not cure the condition and only prolong life and improve quality of life for AIDS patients.

Reverse transcriptase and retroviruses are widely used in genetic engineering. The enzyme is important in recombinant DNA technology. In the future it may be used to insert useful genes into harmless retroviruses which will transfer them to human cells. One example would be to treat babies born with genetic defects caused by a single gene, such as thalassaemia or phenylketonuria, by inserting the missing gene. Gene therapy using a retrovirus has already been used to treat ADA deficiency, which is a rare condition in which children are born with no natural immunity. Before this treatment became available, these children had to live inside a plastic bubble since any contact with pathogens could have killed them.

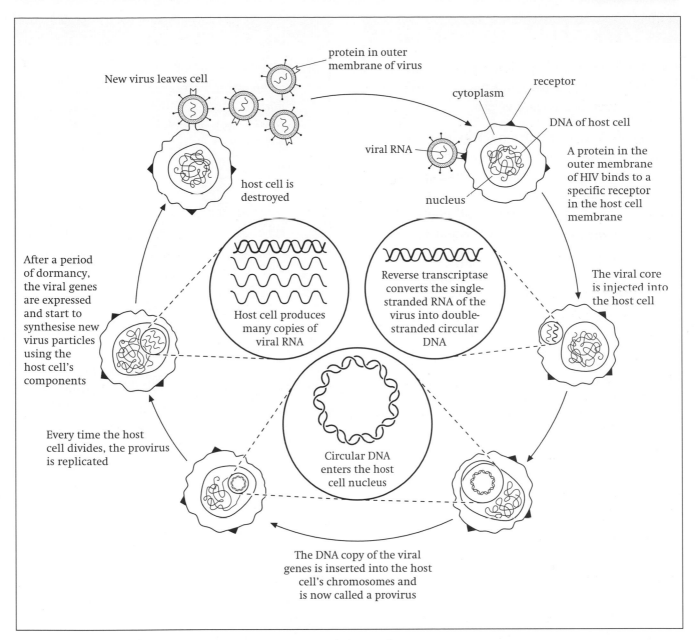

● **Figure 1.23** The life cycle of the human immunodeficiency virus.

SUMMARY

◆ The main groups of microorganisms are the Prokaryotae (bacteria and cyanobacteria), Protoctista, Fungi and viruses.

◆ The Prokaryotae lack a nucleus and membrane-bound organelles. Bacteria are a very diverse group, living in a range of habitats and showing various methods of nutrition. Cyanobacteria are all photo-synthetic and many are nitrogen-fixing.

◆ The Protoctista are all eukaryotic. The group includes four phyla of protozoa, which are all aquatic, unicellular organisms with a variety of locomotory organelles; the Euglenophyta, photosyn-thetic, flagellated unicellular organisms; the Oomycota with non-septate hyphae, and biflagellate asexual spores; and the Chlorophyta, which are unicellular green algae.

◆ The Fungi are also eukaryotic, mainly with chitinous cell walls. This kingdom includes the phyla Zygomycota, Ascomycota and Basidiomycota.

◆ Viruses are obligate parasites which can only reproduce within living cells, so they are not classified as living organisms.

◆ Retroviruses are a group of viruses which have single-stranded RNA as their genetic material and use the enzyme reverse transcriptase to change their RNA to DNA. An example is HIV. Reverse transcriptase and retroviruses are important in genetic engineering.

Questions

1   Make a drawing of a cell of *E. coli* based on the electron micrograph shown in *figure 1.24*. Label all the structures you can identify and annotate your diagram to explain the functions of the parts you have labelled.

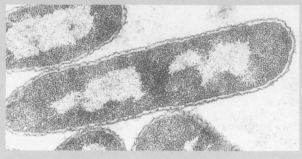

● Figure 1.24

2   Match the following descriptions of genetic material to the correct organism.

Description	Organism
The DNA is double-stranded and not complexed with proteins. It forms a circular loop and there is no nuclear membrane.	yeast
The genetic material may be DNA or RNA but never both. It may be single or double stranded.	bacterium
DNA is double stranded and complexed with proteins. It is organised into chromosomes and enclosed in a nuclear membrane.	virus

● Table 1.9

3   Make a poster to summarise the structures of bacteria, fungi and viruses. Use annotation and colour to show the functions of major structures, and indicate the size range of these organisms.

CHAPTER 2

Techniques used in microbiology and cell culture

By the end of this chapter you should be able to:

By the end of this chapter you should be able to:

1 explain the reasons for safe working practices and the need for risk assessments to be made when using microorganisms;

2 describe the *in vitro* growth requirements of bacteria, fungi and plant cells, with reference to carbon and nitrogen sources, mineral nutrients, temperature, pH and aeration;

3 prepare a nutrient broth and pour nutrient agar plates;

4 use aseptic (sterile) techniques to inoculate solid and liquid media;

5 measure bacterial population growth by means of dilution plating, turbidimetry and use of a haemocytometer;

6 outline the technique of plant tissue culture and explain its importance.

Laboratory safety and aseptic technique

All microbiological cultures should be treated as potentially dangerous; this will lead to good laboratory discipline. In all laboratory work certain precautions are advisable before starting any microbiological work, and aseptic (sterile) techniques should be used throughout the work to reduce the chance of spreading any micro-organisms. These can be carried out as follows.

1 A student or teacher who is unwell should not take part in microbiological exercises. Any cuts or abrasions should be covered with a clean, waterproof dressing.

2 Always wear a laboratory coat for microbiology practical work to protect clothes and reduce the risk of contamination. The coat should be washed after use.

3 There must be no eating, drinking or smoking during practical work.

4 Windows and doors should be kept closed in order to reduce the possibility of airborne contamination.

5 Wash your hands with antibacterial soap before and after microbiological practicals.

6 Wipe down the bench with disinfectant, such as 10% sodium chlorate(I) or 1% Virkon cleaner, before and after microbiological work.

7 Report any spillages of cultures or breakages to your teacher immediately. Pour 10% sodium chlorate(I) on any minor spillages and leave for 10 minutes before wiping with a disposable cloth.

8 Never pipette cultures by mouth, and avoid all hand-to-mouth operations, such as putting your fingers in your mouth or chewing the top of your pen, so as not to accidentally ingest microbes.

9 Tape petri dishes securely after inoculation and label the base clearly with your name, date and nature of the inoculum. This will

avoid microorganisms escaping into the environment should the dish be dropped, and speed the identification of any pathogens involved if contamination does occur.

10 Always work in the vicinity of a bunsen burner. This makes it more convenient to sterilise instruments. It also creates an updraft of air, which helps to prevent microorganisms from the worker being transferred to the culture. Sterilise all implements before use. Metal instruments, such as wires and loops, should be heated to red heat before and after every contact with microorganisms. Glass instruments, such as spreaders, should be dipped in 70% alcohol and the alcohol burned off. Cotton wool bungs or petri dish lids should not be laid on the bench, but held while the vessel is being used. The necks of all tubes, bottles or flasks should be passed through the bunsen flame before and after all operations.

11 Never incubate microbiological cultures at temperatures above 30 °C as this would be approaching the ideal temperature of 37 °C for human pathogens. Never examine live cultures of bacteria and do not open dishes of bacteria once colonies have grown. Colonies contain millions of bacteria so, if pathogens have been accidentally cultured along with the desired organism, they will now be present in very large numbers. Do not isolate organisms from sources of potential pathogens, such as soil, meat, nasal secretions or lavatory seats.

12 Sterilise all media and containers by autoclaving before use. Dispose of all cultures in plastic petri dishes by placing them, unopened, in an autoclavable plastic bag and autoclave at 103 kPa, 121 °C for 20 minutes. Used instruments, such as pipettes, should be placed in disinfectant after use.

Before doing any microbiological work, a **risk assessment** should be carried out. This means that you need to think carefully about any potential hazards in the technique you wish to use. You should try to minimise any possible risk. For example, you should use bacteria that are non-pathogenic. If a chemical you intend to use has a hazard rating, see if you can use a safer alternative chemical. Your tutor will be able to refer you to suitable sources of information.

	Requirement	Functions
From water (a major component of any culture medium)	hydrogen	component of cellular water and organic cell materials
	oxygen	component of cellular water, organic cell materials, electron acceptor in aerobic organisms
Major nutrients	carbon	component of organic cell materials
	nitrogen	component of proteins, nucleic acids and coenzymes
	sulphur	component of some amino acids and coenzymes
	phosphorus	component of nucleic acids, phospholipids and coenzymes
Macronutrients (always included as salts in culture media)	potassium	major inorganic cation, cofactor for certain enzymes
	magnesium	important cellular cation, cofactor for many enzymes, including those involving ATP synthesis, binding of enzymes to substrates, component of chlorophylls
	calcium	important cellular cation, cofactor of some enzymes
	iron	component of cytochromes and some other conjugated proteins, cofactor for certain enzymes
Micronutrients (often present in adequate amounts as contaminants)	manganese	cofactor for some enzymes, sometimes replaces magnesium
	cobalt	component of vitamin B_{12} and coenzymes derived from it
	copper, zinc, molybdenum	inorganic components of special enzymes

NB Some microorganisms have special needs not covered by this table. For example, diatoms (a type of alga) need silica for their cell walls. Sodium is needed by blue-greens and photosynthetic bacteria.

● **Table 2.1** Requirements for the growth of microorganisms.

Nutritional requirements

Organisms need nutrients to generate energy and synthesise cell materials. These nutrients must be obtained from their environment. A **culture medium** must contain all the necessary nutrients in sufficient amount, but microorganisms vary in their requirements. Their general needs are summarised in *table 2.1* opposite.

Carbon

Photoautotrophs and chemoautotrophs use carbon dioxide as their carbon source; other nutritional groups (heterotrophs) need organic carbon (*table 2.2*). Microorganisms are so varied that there is no naturally produced organic compound that cannot be used as a carbon and energy source by at least some microorganisms. Some individual microorganisms may be extremely versatile in their carbon requirements, whilst others can be highly specialised. For example some *Pseudomonas* species are able to use more than 90 organic compounds as their sole carbon and energy source; by contrast, certain cellulose-digesting bacteria can only use cellulose.

Nitrogen and sulphur

Some microorganisms can fix atmospheric nitrogen. Most photosynthetic organisms assimilate nitrogen and sulphur as nitrates and sulphates. Many non-photosynthetic bacteria and fungi can do this too. Some microorganisms need the ammonium ion as their nitrogen source rather than nitrate. Certain microorganisms cannot assimilate sulphate, and therefore need sulphide or an organic compound containing sulphur, such as the amino acid cysteine. The nitrogen and sulphur requirement is often met by organic nutrients, such as amino acids or peptides. These can also form the carbon and energy source.

Growth factors

Growth factors are substances which a microorganism cannot synthesise from simpler substances and which are needed in small amounts for the cell to use in synthesising organic cell materials. They can be subdivided into three groups:

1 amino acids needed for protein synthesis;
2 purines and pyrimidines needed for nucleic acid synthesis;
3 vitamins needed for prosthetic groups or active centres of certain enzymes.

Oxygen

All cells contain oxygen atoms as part of water molecules, and water is provided in all culture media. However, many organisms also need molecular oxygen, O_2, for aerobic respiration. Obligate anaerobes, on the other hand, may be killed or inhibited by molecular oxygen. Filtered, sterile air can be bubbled through a liquid medium to provide a good oxygen supply.

Energy source	Carbon source	
	Inorganic	Organic
Chemical	**Chemoautotrophs** These organisms use carbon dioxide and other inorganic materials as their energy source from oxidation or reduction reactions. Examples: *Nitrobacter* and *Nitrosomonas* in the nitrogen cycle	**Chemoheterotrophs** These organisms use complex organic materials for their carbon and energy sources. Examples: most bacteria, fungi, protoctists and all higher animals
Light	**Photoautotrophs** These organisms use energy from sunlight to fix carbon dioxide which is their carbon source, that is photosynthesis. Examples: all green plants, cyanobacteria, Chlorophyta e.g. *Chlorella*, and some bacteria	**Photoheterotrophs** These organisms use sunlight as their energy source, but complex organic materials as their carbon source. Examples: the purple non-sulphur bacteria, e.g. *Rhodospirillum*

● **Table 2.2** The nutritional categories of living organisms.

Culture media

A culture medium must contain a balanced mixture of the required nutrients, at concentrations sufficient to allow a good growth rate. If a nutrient is in excess, it can inhibit growth or even be toxic. Often one nutrient is present in limiting quantities, to allow adequate growth while preventing the microorganisms from multiplying at their maximum rate. By moderately slowing down the growth rate, the microorganisms are kept healthy. Usually a mineral base is made, containing all the possible nutrients in inorganic form. To this can be added a carbon source, energy source, nitrogen source and growth factors, to suit the organism being cultured. A medium composed entirely of chemically defined nutrients is called a **synthetic medium**. A medium which contains some ingredients of unknown chemical composition, such as malt extract, is called a **complex medium**.

Complex media are very good for growing a wide range of microorganisms, or when the exact nutritional requirements of a microorganism are not known. A medium may be satisfactory for initial growth, but microorganisms change the pH of the medium as they grow, because their metabolic waste products accumulate. To counteract this buffers are often added. Buffer solutions will maintain the pH at a constant level. If the pH changes over a period of time, this may cause denaturation of the microorganism's enzymes, and inhibit growth. As well as a satisfactory culture medium, factors such as light, oxygen and carbon dioxide are often necessary to meet the needs of individual microorganisms.

Selective media

A **selective medium** is suitable for the growth of a specific organism. This means that if you inoculate it with a mixed culture, only the specific organism the medium was designed for will be able to grow on it. Other types of microorganism will be suppressed. Such media are very specialised and are useful in diagnostic work, such as in hospitals or veterinary laboratories. For example a faecal sample containing an assortment of microorganisms can be used to inoculate selective media, such as McConkey agar containing bile salts. If any bacteria grow in this medium, which is selective for salmonellae, then the doctors are alerted to the presence of a pathogen among the many normal bacteria and can prescribe a suitable drug.

SAQ 2.1

The following is a recipe for nutrient broth, a medium used to culture bacteria.

10 g meat extract, 10 g peptone, 5 g NaCl, dissolved in 1 dm^3 (litre) tap water. The pH is adjusted to pH 7.4 using 1 $mol\,dm^{-3}$ sodium hydroxide or 1 $mol\,dm^{-3}$ hydrochloric acid and the medium is dispensed to suitable containers and autoclaved.

a Is this a synthetic or complex medium? Explain.
b What is the carbon source?
c What is the nitrogen source?
d Suggest why tap water is used instead of distilled water.
e Why is it necessary to adjust the pH?

SAQ 2.2

Below are two recipes for fungal media. Read the recipes, then answer the questions below.

Potato dextrose agar
■ Wash 200 g of sound potato tubers, slice and boil in tap water until soft.
■ Crush the boiled tissue in water; when cool, strain through muslin.
■ Make up to 500 cm^3 with distilled water.
■ Add 20 g glucose.
■ Melt 20 g plain agar in another 500 cm^3 water, mix with potato and glucose solution.
■ Dispense to containers and autoclave.

Czapek-Dox medium
0.01 g zinc sulphate, 0.5 g magnesium sulphate, 2.0 g sodium nitrate, 0.5 g potassium chloride, 0.01 g iron(II) sulphate, 1.0 g potassium phosphate, 30.0 g sucrose, 0.005 g copper(II) sulphate, 15.0 g plain agar, all dissolved in 1 dm^3 (litre) of tap water.
a For each of the two media:
   (i) state whether it is a synthetic or complex medium;
   (ii) explain the nutritional function of each ingredient.

b Given a fungus which will grow equally well in both media, which medium would you choose to investigate:

(i) the nutritional requirements of the fungus,

(ii) the conditions necessary for spore formation,

(iii) the effect of pH on the growth of the fungus,

(iv) the range of carbon sources which the fungus is able to utilise,

(v) the effect of temperature on the growth rate of the fungus?

In each case, explain clearly your reasons for choosing that particular medium.

The production of sterilised nutrient media

Nutrient agar is usually prepared and autoclaved (*figure 2.1*) in conical flasks with a non-absorbent cotton wool plug, held in place by aluminium foil or greaseproof paper and an elastic band. It is available in either powder or tablet form. Usually 5 cm^3 of distilled or deionised water is added to each tablet, and normally two tablets with 10 cm^3 of water are needed to produce a slope in a McCartney bottle or a universal bottle. The exact amount of nutrient agar powder varies with the manufacturer and different nutrient media need different amounts of distilled water. You will need to refer to the instructions on the container.

SAQ 2.3

Why, once the water is added to the tablets in the McCartney bottle, should they be allowed to stand for 10–15 minutes before autoclaving?

The equipment and media to be used should be autoclaved to ensure the complete destruction of all forms of living organisms.

The total sterilisation time required varies, and the time taken is made up of three components:

1 penetration time, which is the time taken for the least accessible part of the load to reach the required temperature;

2 holding time, which is the minimum time that, at a given temperature, is known to kill all living organisms, including fungal and bacterial spores;

3 safety time, which is a safety margin and usually half the holding time.

For normal school use the total sterilisation time working at 121 °C and 103 kPa would be 20 minutes.

On autoclaving, the media will boil and enough space must be allowed so that the bubbles do not reach the plug of non-absorbent cotton wool. To prevent excessive moisture from inside the autoclave reaching the cotton wool plug, a greaseproof paper cover held by an elastic band is placed over the plug. An alternative is to use a piece of aluminium foil.

Before use, a volume of water is added to the autoclave, normally enough to fill up to the bottom plate or trivet. The equipment and media (contained in glassware) to be sterilised are placed in a metal container or basket that rests on the trivet. The lids of McCartney bottles should be left loose so they do not explode. The autoclave lid is then securely fastened into place and the heater turned on. Steam should flow continuously through the outlet valve for about one minute to drive off all the air from inside the autoclave. The presence of any air inside the autoclave will lower the final temperature and result in impaired efficiency of the sterilisation process.

SAQ 2.4

Once the steam has built up to the required maximum pressure, excess steam will escape. Why is it necessary to turn down the heat so that the weight vibrates with only a small burst of steam?

Once the material has been autoclaved for the required time the heat is removed and the whole autoclave is allowed to cool down. To test that the pressure has returned to normal

● **Figure 2.1** An autoclave.

atmospheric level, the weight on the central valve should be lifted carefully. Any sign of steam or a hissing noise indicates that the autoclave has not yet cooled enough. If the weight is removed too early, before the pressure is normal and the temperature is 100 °C then any liquid in the autoclave will start to boil. This boiling can cause the medium to froth and stick to the bottle top or cotton wool plug, and in severe cases may boil over and down the outside of the bottle.

If the medium is in McCartney bottles, their lids should be tightened before being removed from the autoclave. If slopes are required, they should be left at a suitable angle for the contents to set. When the medium has solidified, the bottles can be stood upright. The slope increases the surface area for the growth of microorganisms. Slopes are commonly used for keeping stock cultures.

SAQ 2.5 _____
When the nutrient agar has been sterilised by autoclaving, what further procedures are required to produce the agar slopes?

To prepare sterile nutrient agar plates

Nutrient agar is poured into petri dishes while still molten. Agar starts to solidify below 42 °C. It is best to pour the agar below 50 °C and obviously above 42 °C. A good test is to hold the flask in the palm of the hand: when it is just cool enough to handle comfortably it is at an ideal temperature to pour into sterile petri dishes. At this temperature the agar solidifies very quickly, with little condensation on the petri dish lid.

Work in the vicinity of a bunsen burner, with a roaring flame, on a clean surface. Place the sterile petri dishes in a row and lift the petri dish lids just enough to pour in the molten agar. It should reach about half-way up each dish (figure 2.2). Replace the lids quickly and pass the neck of the flask through the bunsen flame for 2–3 seconds after pouring. Hold the plug between the third and the little finger during the whole operation and do not put it down on the bench, but discard it into disinfectant.

SAQ 2.6 _____
The nutrient agar in the flask will cool down. At what temperature does the agar solidify and what simple test can be performed to estimate the temperature?

SAQ 2.7 _____
Why is the neck of the flask flamed?

SAQ 2.8 _____
When the nutrient agar is cool enough to make plates, what precautions need to be taken to reduce the risk of contamination?

SAQ 2.9 _____
Why is it advisable not to use agar plates in which molten agar has splashed over the lid or between the lid and base of the petri dish?

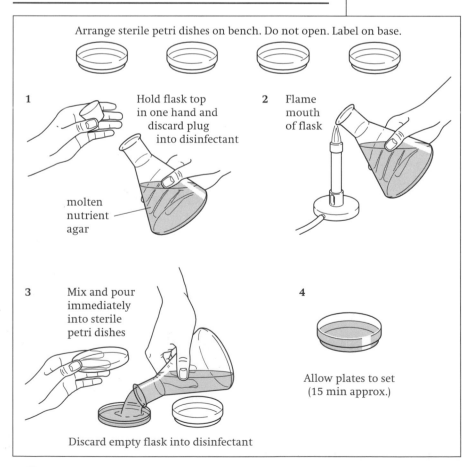

Arrange sterile petri dishes on bench. Do not open. Label on base.

1   Hold flask top in one hand and discard plug into disinfectant

molten nutrient agar

2   Flame mouth of flask

3   Mix and pour immediately into sterile petri dishes

4   Allow plates to set (15 min approx.)

Discard empty flask into disinfectant

● **Figure 2.2** Pouring sterile agar plates.

Other sterilisation methods

■ Filtration is used for liquids that cannot be heat sterilised, such as serum, which is blood plasma with the fibrinogen removed so that it does not clot. The liquid is sucked through a sterile filter pad which traps any microorganisms. The pad is then re-sterilised and discarded.

■ Dry heat is effective and widely used in the flaming of inoculation loops. The nichrome loop is placed in the hot part of the bunsen flame until it glows red along its length. It is then allowed to cool without contact with any surface. Hot air methods using an oven may be used to sterilise glassware, but high temperatures and long times are needed, such as 140°C to 180°C for 1.5–2 hours.

■ Chemicals can be used, but they only kill vegetative cells not endospores. These are used to swab down benches before and after microbiological work. Various types of disinfectant are available.

■ Radiation is used to sterilise plastic equipment. Gamma rays are used commercially for syringe and petri dish sterilisation. Ultraviolet light is particularly effective in killing bacteria and airborne fungal spores. It is used to sterilise transfer chambers, which are special cabinets used for microbiological work in many laboratories.

SAQ 2.10

Why are plastic petri dishes and syringes not sterilised using an autoclave?

Inoculating solid and liquid media

After preparing sterile agar plates or liquid culture media, they can be inoculated with a sample of the microorganisms that are to be cultured. At all times aseptic technique should be followed.

Figure 2.3 shows the preparation of a **streak plate** on agar. A sterile loop is used to streak a

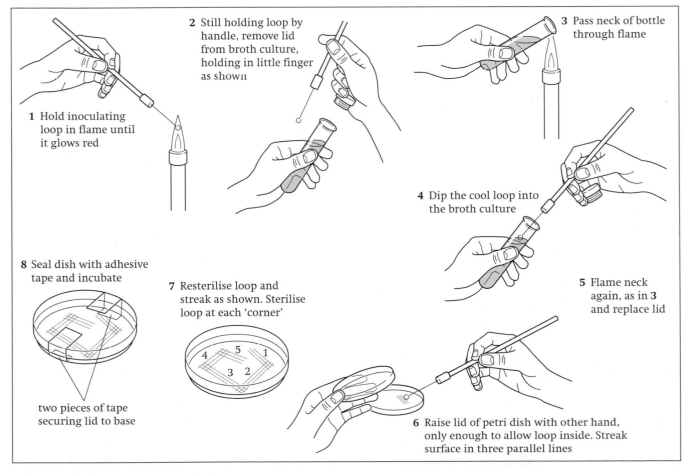

1 Hold inoculating loop in flame until it glows red

2 Still holding loop by handle, remove lid from broth culture, holding in little finger as shown

3 Pass neck of bottle through flame

4 Dip the cool loop into the broth culture

5 Flame neck again, as in 3 and replace lid

6 Raise lid of petri dish with other hand, only enough to allow loop inside. Streak surface in three parallel lines

7 Resterilise loop and streak as shown. Sterilise loop at each 'corner'

8 Seal dish with adhesive tape and incubate

two pieces of tape securing lid to base

● **Figure 2.3** Preparing a streak plate.

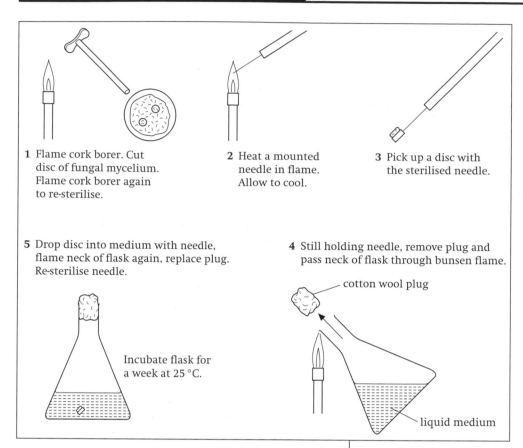

1 Flame cork borer. Cut disc of fungal mycelium. Flame cork borer again to re-sterilise.

2 Heat a mounted needle in flame. Allow to cool.

3 Pick up a disc with the sterilised needle.

5 Drop disc into medium with needle, flame neck of flask again, replace plug. Re-sterilise needle.

4 Still holding needle, remove plug and pass neck of flask through bunsen flame.

cotton wool plug

Incubate flask for a week at 25 °C.

liquid medium

● **Figure 2.4** Inoculating a flask with a mycelial disc.

sample of microorganisms across the surface of the agar in three parallel lines. The loop is then flamed and used to draw three more parallel lines out from the end of the first three. This is repeated three more times, after which the loop is sterilised again.

After inoculation, the lid of the petri dish should be taped on securely using two pieces of tape, as shown in *figure 2.3*. Never place the tape all around the circumference of the dish because this prevents oxygen passing into the dish and creates anaerobic conditions. Since many pathogens are anaerobic, such conditions are hazardous.

Figure 2.4 shows the inoculation of a liquid medium with a fungal mycelial disc.

Growth in bacteria

As bacteria are so small, it is usual to study the growth of populations of bacteria rather than individuals. Growth rate is usually measured as the increase in cell numbers over a measured period of time.

Most bacteria multiply by binary fission, which means that one cell divides into two daughter cells. In this way, the cell number doubles every generation. The time taken for a bacterial population to double in number is called the **generation time**. If conditions are ideal, some bacteria can divide every 20 minutes, although this is rare under normal conditions.

Population growth studies are essential in biotechnological industries using microorganisms on a large scale, such as brewing or producing antibiotics and single cell protein. By studying the growth of microorganisms, the ideal conditions and growth requirements can be found. If microorganisms are cultured in optimum conditions, maximum yield of the product can be obtained.

There are two forms of estimate of cell numbers in a microbial population:

1 a **total cell** count gives the total number of cells present, whether living or dead;

2 a **viable** count takes into account only living cells since these are the only cells capable of dividing.

A sample of a bacterial culture may contain millions of cells, far too many to count. For this reason it is often necessary to make a **serial dilution** of the sample. This is done by aseptically taking $1\,cm^3$ of the bacterial culture and adding it to $9\,cm^3$ of sterile distilled water, to make a 10^{-1} dilution. This is mixed thoroughly, then $1\,cm^3$ of the 10^{-1} dilution is added to $9\,cm^3$ of sterile distilled water to make a 10^{-2} dilution, again mixing thoroughly. This procedure is repeated to give 10^{-3}, 10^{-4} and 10^{-5} dilutions (*figure 2.5*).

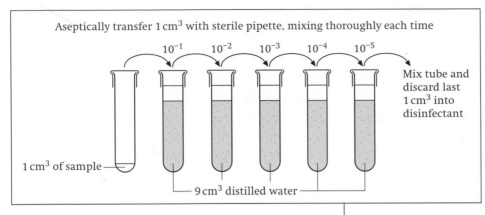

Aseptically transfer 1 cm³ with sterile pipette, mixing thoroughly each time

10^{-1} 10^{-2} 10^{-3} 10^{-4} 10^{-5}

Mix tube and discard last 1 cm³ into disinfectant

1 cm³ of sample

9 cm³ distilled water

● **Figure 2.5** Making a serial dilution.

Total counts

These are made by sampling the culture (usually in liquid medium) at known time intervals and counting the number of cells in a known volume using a counting chamber such as a **haemocytometer** (*figure 2.6*). This is a thick microscope slide, with a slightly thinner central section designed originally for counting blood cells. When a cover slip is placed over the central section, a chamber of known depth (usually 0.1 mm) is formed. The central section is etched with an accurate grid of squares of known size. This allows for the volume of liquid over each square to be calculated. With most standard haemocytometers, this volume is 0.004 mm³.

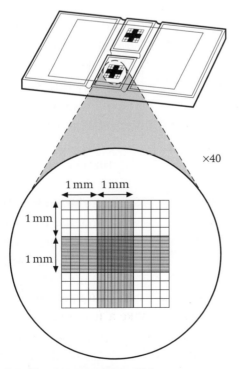

×40

1 mm 1 mm

1 mm

1 mm

● **Figure 2.6** Haemocytometer slide.

A serial dilution of the cell culture is made, and a well-mixed sample of one of the dilutions is introduced into the central chamber with a pipette by carefully allowing the liquid to flow under the cover slip. The sample is viewed under a microscope and the number of microorganisms in several squares is counted. An average is found and, using the dilution factor, the number of microorganisms in the original sample is estimated. There is a rule used to count cells with the haemocytometer, to avoid cells which overlap the lines being counted twice. The rule is only to count cells which overlap the line on the top and left of the square; those to the bottom and right are not counted. This method is particularly useful in studying the population growth of yeast cultures and is used where there are relatively large numbers of cells in the original sample. However it is a *total* cell count. It does not tell us if the cells are alive or dead.

Example In *figure 2.7* there are 9 cells in the square, which has an area of 0.04 mm². The chamber has a depth of 0.1 mm, and therefore there are 9 cells in 0.004 mm³. So in 1 mm³ there are 9/0.004 = 2250 cells.

If the sample from which this was taken had been diluted to a 10^{-5} dilution, then there would be 2250×10^5 cells in 1 mm³ of the original sample and $1000 \times 2250 \times 10^5$ cells in 1 cm³ of the original sample.

Therefore the number of cells in the original sample = 2.25×10^{11} cells per cm³.

Total counts may also be estimated using a colorimeter with a technique known as **turbidimetry**. Increasing the number of cells will make the culture medium more turbid (cloudy), and the turbidity is measured by the colorimeter. A culture sample is thoroughly mixed before being placed in a special flat-sided glass tube called a cuvette. The cuvette then passes before a light in the colorimeter. The amount of light which is absorbed or scattered as it passes through the culture sample is measured to give

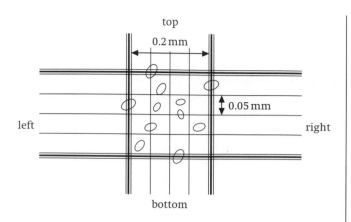

● **Figure 2.7** Total cell count on a haemocytometer grid.

the optical density. The more organisms there are, the less light passes through, so the greater the optical density of the sample.

This method cannot distinguish living cells from dead ones, nor can it distinguish cells from particles of matter in the culture medium, although the colorimeter is usually set to zero before use by using a blank tube containing the culture medium alone.

SAQ 2.11

In *figure 2.8*, find the optical density of the sample. How could you find out the number of cells in a stated volume of this sample?

Viable counts

To obtain a count of viable (live) cells the culture is sampled at known time intervals, and a known volume of sample is diluted with sterile distilled water (usually to give 10^{-1}, 10^{-2}, 10^{-3}, 10^{-4}, 10^{-5} and 10^{-6} dilutions, *figure 2.5*). Each dilution is plated onto sterile nutrient agar using aseptic technique. The plates are usually made in triplicate to increase accuracy. They are incubated until colonies are visible. Since each colony has arisen from a single microorganism, the number of microorganisms in the original sample can be calculated, taking dilution factors into account.

SAQ 2.12

Two students wanted to find out how many yeast cells were present in 1 cm^3 of a culture. Student **A** used a haemocytometer and calculated that there were 2.5×10^4 cells per cm^3. Student **B** made serial dilutions and pour plates, and calculated that there were 1.8×10^3 cells per cm^3. Suggest why the students obtained different answers.

Constructing a growth curve

Because cell numbers are so great, it is hard to plot a graph using actual cell numbers. Therefore, the $\log_{10}$ of the cell number is usually plotted (*figure 2.9*).

The lag phase

During the lag phase there is very little increase in cell numbers though the cells increase in size. Many factors influence the duration of the lag phase, for example:
- if the bacteria are very inactive (such as in the spore stage) they may not divide until conditions are favourable;
- the medium may be quite different from that on which the bacteria were growing previously, so they may

The colorimeter measures the optical density of coloured solutions. When the coloured solution is placed in a special glass tube (a cuvette) in the instrument, light passes through the solution and coloured filter onto the photosensitive element. If the solution is dense, relatively little light passes through; if the solution is clear, more light passes through. The readings on the meter scale vary accordingly.

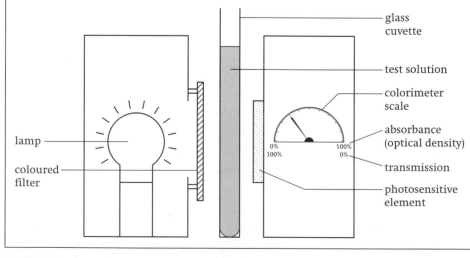

● **Figure 2.8** A colorimeter (spectrophotometer).

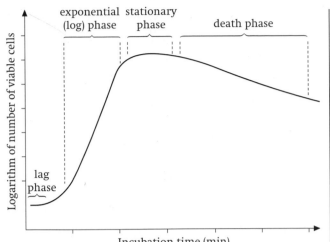

● **Figure 2.9** Generalised growth curve of a bacterial culture.

need to produce new enzymes in order to digest the new nutrients.

The log phase (exponential phase)

In the log phase the bacteria multiply very rapidly because there is no factor limiting their growth. The supply of nutrients, oxygen and all other factors affecting growth are at an optimum, so that numbers double with each generation. For example, if the original inoculum is 10 000 bacteria cm^{-3}:

$$\text{after 1 generation} \quad 10\,000 \times 2 = 10\,000 \times 2^1$$
$$= 20\,000\,\text{cm}^{-3}$$
$$"\quad 2 \text{ generations} \quad 10\,000 \times 2 \times 2 = 10\,000 \times 2^2$$
$$= 40\,000\,\text{cm}^{-3}$$
$$"\quad 3 \text{ generations} \quad 10\,000 \times 2 \times 2 \times 2$$
$$= 10\,000 \times 2^3 = 80\,000\,\text{cm}^{-3}$$
$$"\quad n \text{ generations} \quad 10\,000 \times 2 \times 2 \times 2 \dots$$
$$= 10\,000 \times 2^n$$

Therefore $N = N_0 \times 2^n$

where N_0 = original number of cells
N = number of cells after n generations

The stationary phase

During this phase the population remains stable. The 'birth' rate is approximately balanced by the death rate. If nothing is added to the culture, the amount of nutrients available will now be limiting. The available substrate will provide less energy than the population requires, so the growth rate will slow down. Metabolic products may become toxic as they build up in the medium or the oxygen content may become too low for microorganisms to survive, so increasing the death rate. There may also be a change in pH of the medium, inhibiting enzyme action; for example *Lactobacillus* produces lactic acid from lactose during the souring of milk.

The death phase

In this phase microorganisms are dying rapidly while very few are being produced. Some undergo autolysis, that is enzymes in the microbial cell digest the cell and its contents. This temporarily yields some nutrients for those microorganisms remaining alive, but the cell number falls rapidly.

Continuous cultures

Bacteria grown in batch culture eventually die, as already described, due to such factors as nutrient depletion. However, bacterial cultures can be maintained indefinitely in the exponential phase. This is done by continuing to supply fresh nutrients to the medium and, at the same time, carefully removing toxic wastes and a continuous stream of the microorganisms. It is very difficult to achieve this in the school laboratory but there are many natural examples of continuous culture, the digestive system of the cow being perhaps the best.

Growth in fungi

Unicellular fungi such as yeasts grow in a similar way to bacteria. Filamentous fungi, however, grow by elongation of their hyphae. Their form of growth varies according to the medium on which they are grown.

On a solid medium the fungal mycelium grows as an approximately circular colony across the surface of the medium. Usually the hyphae do not penetrate the medium very deeply because fungi are aerobic and rely on gaseous diffusion through the medium. Colony diameter is usually used as an index of growth.

On a stationary liquid medium the mycelium forms an approximately circular 'felt' or 'mat' on the surface. However, in a rapidly stirred liquid medium the fungus forms pellets of mycelium, which are approximately spherical and spread throughout the medium. To measure growth, the fungus can be filtered off and the dry mass obtained.

Growth curve for a filamentous fungus

Lag phase

As with bacteria, there is a lag phase when no growth occurs (*figure 2.10*). There are various reasons for this:

■ if a spore suspension is used as an inoculum, it will take time for the spores to germinate;
■ if a mycelial disc is used, there will be many damaged hyphae which need to be repaired before they can grow;
■ in either case, new enzymes may need to be synthesised before the fungus can feed off the available nutrients.

Rapid growth phase

The colony diameter, or dry mass of the fungus, increases linearly with time. However, with a fungus, growth is rarely exponential. Like bacteria, fungi grow rapidly at this time due to the presence of optimal conditions including a plentiful supply of nutrients.

Stationary phase

Growth slows down, due to the accumulation of toxic wastes, lack of nutrients, or a physical barrier such as the edge of the petri dish. Sometimes the hyphae in the centre of the mycelium undergo autolysis.

Death phase

The mycelium undergoes autolysis if the culture is maintained long enough.

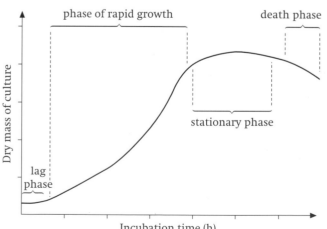

● **Figure 2.10** Growth curve of a filamentous fungus in liquid medium.

Factors affecting microbial growth

Temperature

All living organisms have an optimum temperature for their growth. They can be classified into three categories according to the temperature range in which they grow best.

Thermophiles have an optimum temperature above 40 °C. Thermophiles grow in hot springs, compost heaps, hot water heaters, tropical soils, hot tubs (jacuzzi) and so on. One type of bacterium has been found growing at 250 °C in the hot water streaming from a thermal vent in the ocean floor; the huge pressures at this depth prevent the cytoplasm from boiling and the bacterial proteins have extra chemical bonds to protect them from destabilisation.

Mesophiles grow best between 20 and 40 °C. Most microorganisms fall into this category, including human pathogens, which are adapted to grow at 37 °C.

Psychrophiles (or **cryophiles**) grow actively at temperatures below 20 °C. These organisms grow in deep oceans, in the Arctic and Antarctic, and in fridges and freezers where they cause spoilage of refrigerated and frozen foods.

pH

Most bacteria grow within a pH range of 6–8 and grow best at a neutral pH of 7. Few bacteria can survive at pH values below 4. The human stomach has a pH of 1.5–2.0 which kills most bacteria. The skin and vagina in the adult human are acidic to protect against infection. However, some bacteria can grow at extremes of pH, for example *Thiobacillus thiooxidans* oxidises sulphur to sulphuric acid and can grow at a pH of 0.

Fungi can tolerate acidic conditions although they grow best at pH 5–6. Fungi are very important in the decay of organic matter in acidic soils.

Microorganisms tend to produce waste products that can rapidly alter the pH of the medium. For this reason, buffers are usually added to culture media.

Oxygen

Aerobes require molecular oxygen for their metabolism, whereas anaerobes generally do not.

Some microorganisms require a little oxygen but are harmed if too much or too little is available. Many of these need elevated carbon dioxide levels too. These microorganisms often live in parts of the human body, for example, in the large intestine where low oxygen and high carbon dioxide levels are found. **Facultative anaerobes** grow aerobically when oxygen is present, but have a less efficient alternative mechanism so that they can also function in the absence of oxygen. **Obligate anaerobes** need an oxygen-free atmosphere for their growth. Some anaerobes can survive, although they will not grow, in the presence of oxygen; these are **aerotolerant**. The **strict anaerobes** are killed by even a slight amount of oxygen.

The 'stab' technique may be used to determine the oxygen requirements of a bacterium. Obligate aerobes will only grow on the surface of the agar. Lower down the 'stab' there is less oxygen available as it has to diffuse through the agar. This means that only facultative anaerobes can grow here. This technique is shown in *figure 2.11*.

SAQ 2.13

Explain why, after incubation, the colonies of bacteria growing near the surface are mainly white, but those growing further down are mainly yellow.

Carbon dioxide

Some microorganisms, including many human pathogens, grow best in elevated carbon dioxide levels.

Water potential

Microorganisms must have water available for growth. If the water potential of the medium is higher (less negative) than that of the microbial cell, the microorganism will take up water by osmosis. In bacteria the rigid cell wall helps to resist cell lysis, but lysis can occur in micro-organisms with more fragile cells. Similarly, if the water potential of the environment is much lower (more negative) than that of the microorganism, water leaves the cell by osmosis and the

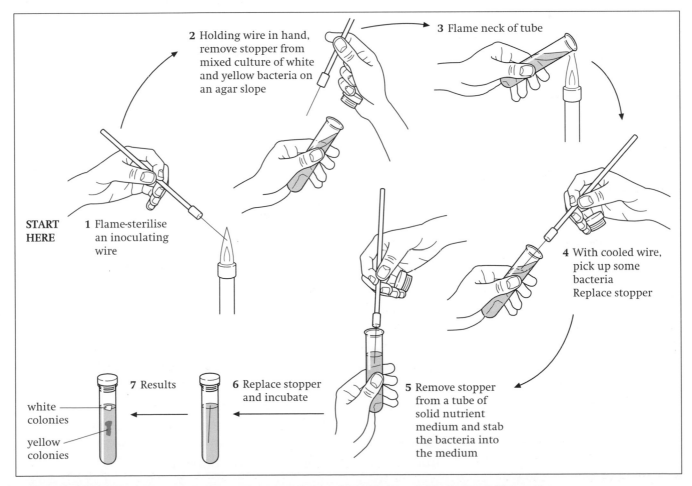

• **Figure 2.11** The 'stab' technique used to determine the oxygen requirements of bacteria.

microorganism may die. This observation has been exploited in food preservation: high levels of either salt or sugar have been used for centuries to preserve food. Some microorganisms are adapted to grow at very low water potentials; these are called **halophiles**.

Light

Photoautotrophs require visible light as an energy source. Some other wavelengths can be used to kill microorganisms. Short wavelength ultraviolet light may be used to kill pathogens in food shops and hospitals. X-rays can be used to sterilise medical equipment such as syringes.

Chemicals

Many chemicals, such as antiseptics and disinfectants, inhibit microbial growth. Antibiotics also affect microbial growth;

these fall into two types, **bacteriostatic**, which prevent bacterial replication, and **bactericidal**, which kill the bacteria.

Nutritional factors

These were discussed earlier (page 25). Lack of any of these nutrients will limit the growth of a microorganism. Each nutrient has an optimum value which will give maximum growth. If a nutrient is supplied at a suboptimum level, there is often a linear relationship between the amount of substrate available and growth rate.

This is the basis of a **bioassay**, a valuable means of measuring the concentrations of substances like vitamins when these are very low. In a bioassay a test bacterium is selected which will only grow in the presence of the vitamin. When the vitamin has been used up, bacterial growth stops. The amount of bacterial growth will therefore be proportional to the concentration of the limiting vitamin, provided all other nutrients are available in excess. A standard curve is made, and from this the amount of vitamins in other substances can be assessed.

SAQ 2.14

Define the following terms:
obligate anaerobe; facultative anaerobe; mesophile; psychrophile.

Growth of bacteriophages

Bacteriophages replicate by means of the lytic cycle and the main features of this can be demonstrated by plotting a 'one-step growth curve'. A broth culture of bacteria is mixed with a suspension of compatible bacteriophage particles, such as *E. coli* with the T2 phage. Quantities are chosen so that the bacteria are in considerable excess. The mixture is incubated for a short while, to allow the phages to become attached to the bacterial cell walls. The mixture is then greatly diluted and incubated again. Samples of known volume are taken at intervals and plated onto agar. The uninfected bacteria will grow as a lawn, but infected bacteria will fail to grow and will leave a clear area in the bacterial lawn known as a 'plaque'. The plaques are counted at each stage to obtain a growth curve (*figure 2.12*). Initially, the plaque count is constant; this is the **latent phase** following adhesion of phages to bacterial cells. As infected bacteria begin to lyse, and new phage particles are released, the plaque count rises abruptly until all the infected cells lyse. This is called the **burst period**. After this lysis has occurred, the plaque count remains approximately constant, since the diluting procedure ensures that few of the released phages will become attached to uninfected bacterial cells. The average number of new phage particles released from each infected cell is called the **burst size**.

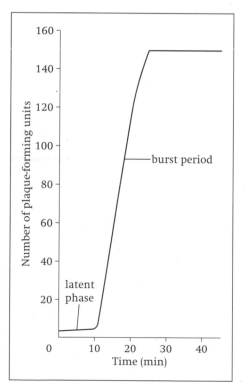

● **Figure 2.12** One-step growth curve of a bacteriophage virus.

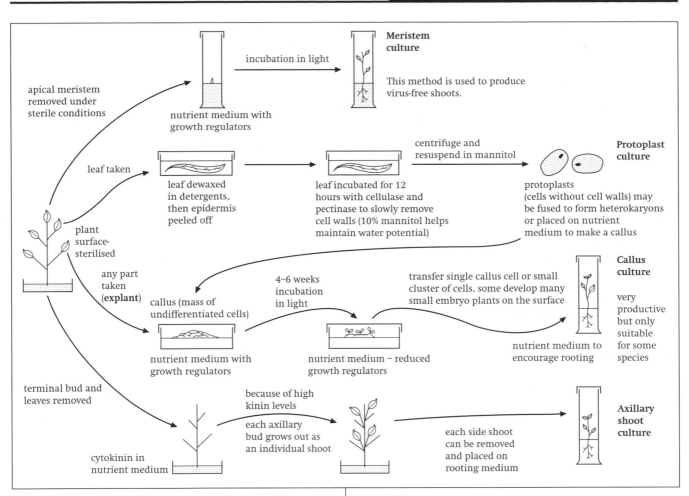

• **Figure 2.13** Plant tissue culture techniques.

Plant tissue culture

Plant tissue culture is now a very important part of biotechnology. This technique involves the regeneration of whole plants from individual cells or small pieces of plant tissue. The new plants produced will be **clones** of the original plant, i.e. they will be genetically identical. Plant cells can be grown in culture as follows:

1 Their cell walls can be removed and the protoplasts grown in a liquid medium, just like fungal or bacterial cultures. This is called **protoplast culture**.

2 Pieces of plant tissue, called **explants**, can be grown on a solid medium. These develop in various ways, depending on the constituents of the medium.

Plant tissue culture methods

A number of different methods are used in plant tissue culture. These are summarised in *figure 2.13*.

It is very important that these techniques are carried out in very strictly aseptic conditions. This is because plant cells divide much more slowly than bacterial or fungal cells, so even one

• **Figure 2.14** Many small plantlets being produced from one piece of plant tissue on a sterile nutrient medium.

contaminating bacterial cell or fungal spore could soon outgrow the cultured plant cells.

Cultures are usually grown in the light at a regulated temperature, normally 20–25 °C (*figure 2.14*).

The importance of plant cell and tissue culture

Micropropagation

It is not always easy to micro-propagate plants as some species respond better than others. The technique is expensive and time-consuming, but there are useful applications. Some valuable trees, such as hybrids or polyploids, are infertile and need vegetative propagation. Tissue culture is a fast method which can produce many small plantlets from just one plant. The Royal Botanical Gardens at Kew are an example of a place where these methods are used to increase numbers of rare and endangered plant species.

Micropropagated plants are disease free and so more desirable for the exchange of plant material between countries, since they eliminate the need for quarantine. Plant breeders have sometimes been surprised to find that when certain plants have been propagated using meristem culture, and are therefore virus-free, they grow far more vigorously than before. These plants had not shown any sign of disease, but nevertheless must have been virus-infected. An example of this is the King Edward variety of potatoes.

See page 55, chapter 4, for more information on creating disease-resistant plants and new hybrids.

Transformation by selected gene transfer

Desirable genes can be inserted into the plant cell, which means that new hybrids can be produced with qualities such as drought resistance or herbicide resistance. One example is the production of crop plants resistant to the weedkiller, glyphosate. If farmers grow such crops, they can use glyphosate to spray their fields. This will destroy

Nutrients	Ingredients	Concentration (mg dm^{-3})
Macronutrients	Ammonium nitrate	1650.0
	Potassium nitrate	1900.0
	Calcium chloride	440.0
	Magnesium sulphate	370.0
	Potassium dihydrogen phosphate	170.0
Chelated iron	Sodium EDTA	37.3
	Iron(II) sulphate	27.8
Micronutrients	Boric acid	6.2
	Manganese sulphate	16.9
	Zinc sulphate	8.6
	Potassium iodide	0.83
	Sodium molybdenate	0.25
	Copper sulphate	0.025
	Cobalt chloride	0.025
Carbon compounds	Sucrose	20 000.0
	Inositol	100.0
Vitamins	Thiamine	0.1

● **Table 2.3** Murashige and Skoog plant cell culture medium. Auxins and kinins are added in appropriate quantities to the above medium in order to stimulate the organ development required. The medium is made up to 1 dm^3 using glass-distilled water. For a solid growth medium, agar is added.

any weeds present without causing damage to the crop. There is more on this in chapter 4.

Production of secondary plant products

Plants produce many useful secondary products, such as digoxin (a heart drug) from the foxglove; codeine (a painkiller) from the opium poppy; spearmint (a flavouring) from mint; and pyrethrin (an insecticide) from chrysanthemum. You can see some more examples in *table 4.1* on page 53. At present, many of these products are imported, so climate, transport difficulties and political instability affect supply. Although research is still at an early stage, it is theoretically possible to grow protoplast cultures in vast fermenters (just like microbial cells) to produce these products on a large scale. In practice, problems occur because protoplasts are so fragile, having no cell walls to protect them.

Plant cell culture media

It is important that the nutrient medium contains the correct balance of plant growth hormones, particularly auxins and kinins. These control the development of callus tissue, roots or shoots, depending on the ratio in which they are present.

A commonly used medium is that of Murashige and Skoog (M and S medium) described in *table 2.3*.

SAQ 2.15 _____

Name the **a** carbon source; **b** nitrogen source(s) in M and S medium used for plant tissue culture.

SAQ 2.16 _____

Plants can photosynthesise. Suggest why a carbon source is necessary in a plant tissue culture medium.

SAQ 2.17 _____

Why is it important that plant tissue culture is carried out under strictly aseptic conditions?

SUMMARY

◆ Various methods are used to sterilise media and microbiological equipment.

◆ Microorganisms need nutrients to generate energy and synthesise cell materials. These nutrients must be provided in the culture media. Selective media only support the growth of a limited range of species.

◆ Growth in bacteria is usually studied by measuring population growth: either the total cell count or the viable cell count may be used. The growth curve for a filamentous fungus involves measuring mycelial growth as either colony diameter or dry mass.

◆ The growth of microorganisms is affected by factors such as pH, oxygen and carbon dioxide availability, water potential, light, chemicals and nutritional factors.

◆ Plant cells can be cultured using plant tissue culture techniques. This has a number of important applications in biotechnology, such as producing many genetically identical small plants from one parent plant.

Questions

1 **a** Use the data in *table 2.4* below to construct a growth curve.
   b Label your graph and discuss the factors which control the growth rate at each stage.
   c The time taken for a bacterial population to double in number is called the **generation time**. Calculate the generation time for *E. coli* using the data from your graph.

Hours	Numbers of viable cells per cm^3 medium	Total number of cells per cm^3 medium
0	20 100	20 100
2	21 500	27 300
4	496 450	560 000
6	5 430 265	6 450 000
8	81 900 500	105 760 500
12	83 405 700	126 350 045
24	80 500 045	127 600 500

● **Table 2.4** Growth of a population of *E. coli* in nutrient broth

2 Account for the differences in the form of growth between a fungus grown on a stationary liquid medium and a fungus grown in an agitated liquid medium.

CHAPTER 3

Large-scale production

By the end of this chapter you should be able to:

1 describe the specialist structural features of laboratories working with microorganisms, which are designed to prevent contamination of workers and the environment;

2 explain what is meant by the terms batch culture and continuous culture and compare their advantages and disadvantages with reference to the production of penicillin and mycoprotein;

3 describe the general structure of a fermenter used for large scale production;

4 explain the major problems associated with the large scale fermentation process as opposed to laboratory production;

5 carry out experiments to show the effects of varying conditions on the growth of microorganisms.

At the beginning of chapter 2, safety guidelines were given for working with microorganisms in the school laboratory. Such safety precautions are also necessary in industry but they are even more strict.

Safety in industrial microbiology

Industrial and research laboratories have a very strict set of guidelines to follow for microbiological work. Laboratory surfaces, such as floors, working surfaces and walls must be smooth and easy to clean. There must be a regular routine of cleaning and maintenance. Some areas are designated 'clean zones' where full protective clothing must be worn (figure 3.1), and careful techniques used to avoid the escape of pathogens or the introduction of contaminating organisms into pure cultures. Often, laminar flow cabinets are used to create a sterile working area. These have air flow hoods which create a more negative air pressure within the cabinet than in the laboratory. This minimises the chances of microorganisms being carried into the laboratory in air currents. The air flow hood filters all air entering and leaving the cabinet.

SAQ 3.1

In many microbiology laboratories there are two doors present at the entrance to provide an air lock. What is the advantage of having such an air lock?

In recent years there have been concerns expressed about potential hazards in the use of genetically engineered organisms, particularly if they are released into the environment. Evidence to date shows that recombinant organisms are no

● **Figure 3.1** Clean room and protective clothing.

more dangerous than traditional ones. However, it is wise for research establishments and companies involved in biotechnology to be extremely careful and be aware of public concerns when designing production facilities (*figure 3.2*).

Fermenters should be designed to keep contaminating organisms out and therefore they should also be effective in retaining any potential pathogens. There are design features on the fermenters, such as double mechanical seals on the agitator shafts and filters on the exhaust gas outlets to help ensure that this is the case. The sampling outlets (ports) must be carefully designed to contain any spillage and must avoid the formation of aerosols (tiny droplets of liquid in the air). Aerosols are a risk because they provide a moist, oxygen-rich environment which encourages the growth of microorganisms. Aerosols can be inhaled and so are an easy route of infection. They can also spray microorganisms over a considerable distance where they can contaminate equipment and laboratory personnel. All effluent from the fermenter and the washings from the cleaning process must be passed through a continuous steriliser or into a large 'kill' tank where disinfectants are added to destroy any remaining microorganisms.

There may also be hazards involved in **downstream processing**, that is the processes required to obtain the product from the contents of the fermenter. Care needs to be taken with heat exchangers to avoid freezing the culture fluid, which could result in thermal expansion and fracture of the exchanger. Centrifuges are notorious for producing aerosols. They must have an air-tight seal and all vents on them should be fitted with microbiological filters. All the equipment must be connected with high quality piping and all joints securely welded. It should be possible to sterilise the whole of the fermenter and downstream processing equipment, usually with steam under pressure.

Aseptic operation

For a successful fermentation, it is vital that there should be no contamination of the culture. For this reason the entire fermenter, all ancillary equipment and the growth medium must be sterile before inoculation. The air supplied during the fermentation must be sterile and there must

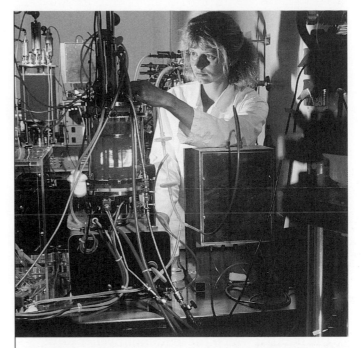

● **Figure 3.2** Researcher investigating conditions for producing recombinant protein in the laboratory.

be no mechanical breaks in the fermenter which might allow microorganisms to enter.

All equipment is cleaned with hot water before use and then sterilised *in situ* with steam. The steam must be able to reach all parts of the fermenter assembly so it is vital that the fermenter is designed to avoid pockets of air which may occur if valves are incorrectly sited. All the interior surfaces should be polished since rough surfaces can act as a reservoir for contaminating microorganisms.

The culture medium, which can be several thousand dm^3, may be heat sterilised in the fermenter itself by passing steam through the cooling coils and jacket. Alternatively the medium may be prepared in a separate vessel and passed through a continuous steriliser.

All additives, for example an antifoaming agent, must also be sterilised, though strong acids or alkalis added to adjust the pH do not need sterilisation. The air supply to the culture medium is sterilised by filtration. Many types of filter materials have been developed to trap microorganisms. Filtration can remove bacteria and fungi but bacteriophages in the air cannot be removed this way and their presence could result in the loss of an entire culture. In some cases, therefore, the air is heated to inactivate any bacteriophages and then cooled again before it enters the vessel. A fermentation plant designed for the large-scale production of human growth hormone or of insulin, both of which use recombinant *E. coli*, must not be situated downwind of a farmyard or sewage plant which are both rich sources of coliphages (bacteriophages that infect *E. coli*).

SAQ 3.2

Why are bacteriophages a serious problem if they infect an industrial fermenter?

Air leaving the fermenter must also be sterilised, particularly if recombinant organisms are being grown. Not only is this a safety requirement, but it also prevents key microbial strains from becoming available to competitor companies. Filtration is used to sterilise the air.

The point at which the agitator/impeller driveshaft enters the vessel is a potential source of contamination, so double mechanical seals are used and the moving parts are lubricated with condensed steam to maintain sterility.

SAQ 3.3

Explain the reasons for the following.
a A traditional brewery, using open-topped fermenters, provides a footbath containing disinfectant by the door leading to the fermenters.
b A yogurt factory prepares fruit by sterilising it and sealing it in large drums. The fruit is removed from the drum when required by pumping in sterile air.
c A supermarket has ultraviolet lights in its delicatessen area.

SAQ 3.4

You are asked to design a new microbiology laboratory for a local hospital. Describe three structural features that you would include to promote microbiological safety in the new laboratory.

Methods of culture

Solid substrate

This is probably the oldest method of culturing microorganisms, and involves growing them on a solid or semi-solid substrate. Examples are grow-

ing mushrooms on compost, breadmaking, silage production, cheese production, sauerkraut and tempe kedele (fermented soybean curd) production. Non-food examples include the production of methane from sewage sludge and other waste.

Aqueous culture

This refers to culture in a substrate which has a high water content. There are two methods: batch and continuous fermentation.

Batch culture

This is carried out in a **closed** or **batch fermenter** (*figure 3.3*). The microorganism is put into the fermenter with a nutrient medium and left for the process to take place. The product is separated from the rest of the mixture at the end. While the process is going on, nothing is added to the vessel and nothing is removed, except for the venting of waste gases. A typical growth curve for a batch culture is shown in *figure 2.9*, page 33. Note that all nutrients are depleted at the end of the process.

During a batch culture, environmental factors are constantly changing although temperature is usually controlled. The phase of exponential growth lasts for only a short time.

A variation on batch culture is a **fed-batch process**, where nutrients are added at intervals during the fermentation.

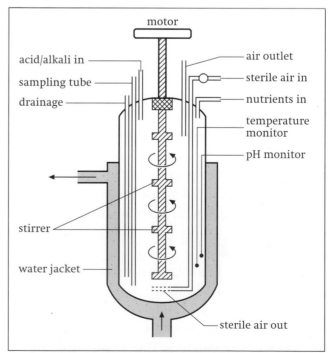

● **Figure 3.3** Section through a batch fermenter.

Advantages of a batch culture compared with a continuous process are that:

- it is easy to set up and control the environmental factors;
- vessels are versatile: they may be used for different processes at different times, enabling a manufacturer to meet market demands more easily;
- should a culture become contaminated, only one batch is lost, so the cost to the manufacturer is minimised.

Continuous culture

Continuous culture takes place in **open fermenters**, so that nutrients can be added continuously, at a steady rate, to exactly balance the amount of product being removed. This maintains the microorganisms in an **exponential** phase of growth. It is vital to monitor the environmental factors, namely pH, oxygen level, nutrient concentration and accumulation of products, and to keep these constant.

Advantages of continuous culture (and consequently, disadvantages of batch culture) are that:

- smaller vessels are needed because the process is more productive, with the microorganisms being maintained in exponential growth;
- this greater productivity can be more cost-effective.

However, there are disadvantages. In practice:

- it is very difficult to monitor all the environmental factors and the system can become unbalanced (should a continuous culture break down, there is considerable waste, which is costly);
- there can be practical problems, like foaming, clumping of cells and microbial growth blocking inlets.

SAQ 3.5

Look at *figure 3.3*. What are the functions of the following parts?

a stirrer **b** water jacket
c acid/alkali inlet **d** sterile air inlet
e air outlet

SAQ 3.6

What shape would you expect for the growth curve of a microorganism grown in a continuous fermenter?

Setting up an industrial process

It is not always straightforward to scale up a laboratory process to a profitable and efficient industrial process. To do this, three stages are involved.

Laboratory-scale

The researcher uses a small laboratory flask with a volume of, say, 200 cm³ to grow a microorganism which has been found to make a useful product (*figure 3.2*). The optimum conditions for growth of the organism are determined and, if the process works smoothly, the next stage is to scale up the process into a bigger vessel.

Pilot plant-scale

The microorganism is cultured in a small-scale fermenter of 200–500 dm³ (litres) in volume (*figure 3.4*). This is to find the optimum operating conditions, which may not be the same as they were for very small-scale growth.

Industrial plant-scale

The microorganism is grown in a massive industrial fermenter which is thousands of dm³ in volume. However, there are many problems. One important problem is in cooling the vessel. The 200 cm³ vessel is stirred by a small electric mixer, using only

● **Figure 3.4** Small-scale industrial fermentation.

a small amount of electricity (typically about 300 W) so there will be few problems in cooling the vessel sufficiently. If it were scaled up directly in proportion to the vessel, the mixer would be the size of a tower block, use 150 MW of electricity and generate enough heat to vaporise the contents of the fermenter. So a different method of mixing is needed.

Other problems involved in scaling up the process are that:

- the heating up and cooling down of a large volume of liquid is very slow;
- sterile conditions are vital and the fermenter must stay sterile, since the loss of even one contaminated batch would be costly;
- it is more difficult when dealing with large volumes to maintain constant flavour and quality;
- all the processing after fermentation, such as filtering, drying, distillation, extraction and waste treatment, must be carried out on a large scale;
- any error could lead to the loss of several days' production or even wrecked equipment.

For these reasons, chemical engineers must undertake sophisticated calculations and take into account many different factors when designing a full-scale production plant.

Antibiotic production

Alexander Fleming's accidental discovery of the antibiotic penicillin in 1929 is well known. He found the mould *Penicillium notatum* contaminating a petri dish of pathogenic bacteria and inhibiting their growth. From this he isolated penicillin. However, it was not until the Second World War that penicillin was successfully produced on a large scale. At first, the mould *Penicillium* was grown in static liquid culture in various flasks, shallow pans and milk bottles, but this process was highly inefficient and it was not possible to produce enough penicillin to meet demand. Later, a strain was developed which would grow submerged in the medium and give better yields. Modern production of penicillin uses a mutant strain of *Penicillium* developed in the laboratory.

An **antibiotic** can be defined as 'a chemical substance produced by a microorganism that, in dilute solution, can exert a growth-inhibiting effect on other microorganisms'. This definition is sometimes considered to be rather narrow since it leaves out the sulphonamides which are synthesised chemically but operate similarly to antibiotics.

Scientists are not sure why microorganisms produce antibiotics. It seems unlikely that they produce antibiotics to fight natural enemies, as so few species possess this ability and the antibiotics are not produced until late in the microorganism's life cycle. Two theories have been proposed to explain antibiotic production.

1 Antibiotics are secondary metabolites, that is they are produced after the main growth phase is over. They may be produced to keep enzyme systems operative when the microorganism has run out of nutrients and cell division is no longer possible. Normally, when the substrate has been used up, the enzymes of that particular pathway would be broken down. If a new nutrient supply was found, there would be a delay while the necessary enzymes were produced. It has been suggested that making a secondary metabolite keeps the enzymes active, so that the microorganism can quickly take advantage of any new food supply.

2 Antibiotic production may be a means of ridding the cell of metabolic waste. Although not toxic to the organism producing them, the waste could still be highly toxic to other microorganisms and thus act as an antibiotic. If the toxin phenylacetic acid is added to a culture of *Penicillium*, penicillin production is increased, which supports this theory. It is of course possible that both theories are correct since they are not contradictory.

Industrial production of antibiotics

The first stage of antibiotic production is screening for microorganisms which produce antibiotics (*figure 3.5*). Many such organisms have been found in soil, although other sources have also been useful.

Once an antibiotic has been found, it must be tested to find its optimum production conditions (such as temperature and pH). Chromatography and other techniques can be used to see whether one or more compounds are produced. This method also indicates whether the antibiotic is

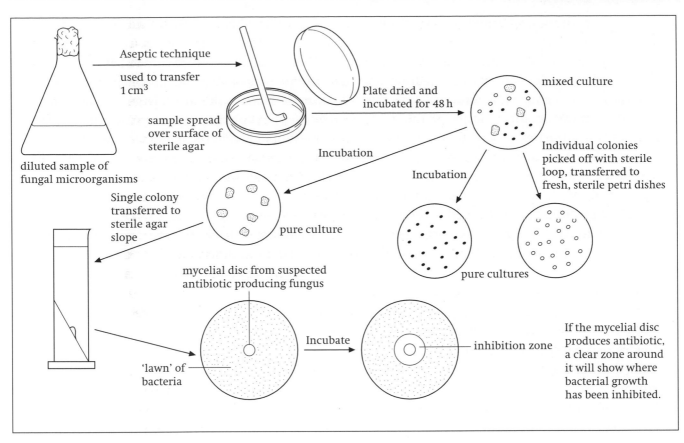

● **Figure 3.5** Screening for antibiotics in a fungus.

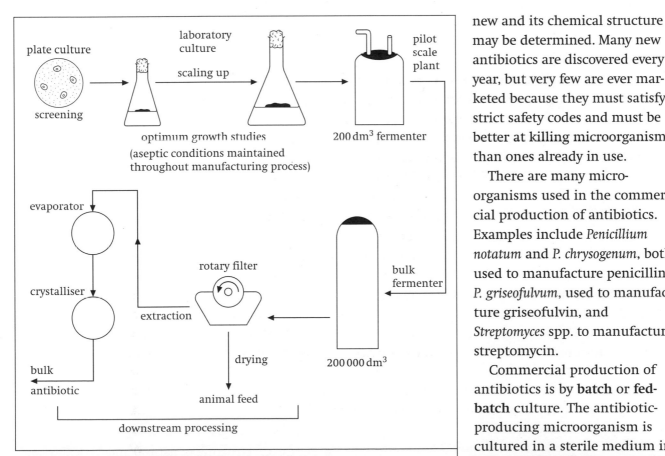

● **Figure 3.6** Commercial antibiotic production, e.g. penicillin.

new and its chemical structure may be determined. Many new antibiotics are discovered every year, but very few are ever marketed because they must satisfy strict safety codes and must be better at killing microorganisms than ones already in use.

There are many microorganisms used in the commercial production of antibiotics. Examples include *Penicillium notatum* and *P. chrysogenum*, both used to manufacture penicillin, *P. griseofulvum*, used to manufacture griseofulvin, and *Streptomyces* spp. to manufacture streptomycin.

Commercial production of antibiotics is by **batch** or **fed-batch** culture. The antibiotic-producing microorganism is cultured in a sterile medium in a vast fermenter (*figure 3.6*). It is grown under optimum conditions of temperature and pH (as determined by the pilot study) so that the organism grows and produces the antibiotic and secretes it into the medium. The medium contains sugar, such as glucose, together with all the other nutrients the organism needs to grow, such as nitrates and sulphates. Fermentation is aerobic, so sterile air must be added to the fermenter. The fermentation is monitored so that the culture is stopped when the maximum level of antibiotic is present. The medium is then filtered off and the antibiotic extracted. The spent microorganisms are sometimes used for animal feed.

SAQ 3.7

a Suggest the purpose of the initial plate culture.

b In the laboratory-scale process, the optimum conditions for growth of the microorganism are studied. What kinds of conditions might affect growth?

c In the bulk fermentation stage, these conditions need to be controlled. For each condition you have listed in **b** state how it might be controlled in the bulk fermenter.

d Suggest how the bulk fermenter, and other equipment used to manufacture antibiotics in bulk, might be sterilised.

e Why is it undesirable to keep a sample of each bulk fermentation to inoculate future fermentation runs?

f Suggest advantages and disadvantages of using antibiotic waste for animal feed.

Penicillin production

Penicillin is one of the best known and most widely used antibiotics. A system has been developed for producing penicillin called **cyclic fed-batch culture (CFBC)**. In this process, fresh nutrients are continually added at a very slow rate, and some of the culture is removed. This is because antibiotics are produced in the greatest quantity when the fungus is kept short of nutrients. If the fungus receives too many nutrients, the population grows densely but does not produce antibiotics, but if there is a lack of nutrients the culture will die.

Penicillium chrysogenum is grown in a $200\,000\,dm^3$ fermenter in a liquid medium containing a mixture of glucose and lactose, with a nitrogen source such as yeast extract. A buffer is also added, to keep the pH at about 6.5. *Penicillium* grows better on glucose, but produces more penicillin when fed on lactose. It takes 5–8 days to produce a large amount of antibiotic. The contents of the fermenter are filtered. The antibiotic is in the liquid medium. There is then a chemical extraction process, during which potassium ions are added, so that the penicillin precipitates out as the potassium salt. It is then washed, filtered and dried.

Sometimes antibiotics are chemically modified after fermentation. For instance, all naturally occurring penicillins have a common ring structure as shown in *figure 3.7*. Different forms of penicillin have different acyl side-chains. The *Penicillium* strains first used to manufacture penicillin largely produced penicillin F. Then it was found that adding corn steep liquor to the medium caused a different kind of penicillin to be synthesised, that is penicillin G. Corn steep liquor contains a precursor of phenylacetic acid, which in turn forms the acyl side-chain of penicillin G. Penicillin G is much more useful clinically than penicillin F, so adding phenylacetic acid to the growing cultures has now become part of the

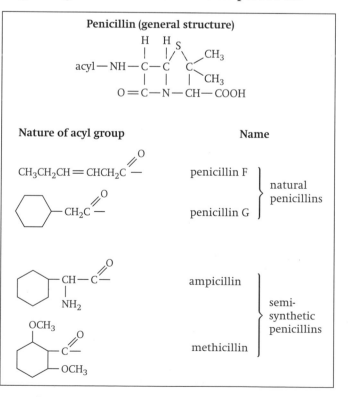

● **Figure 3.7** Structure of natural and synthetic penicillins.

production process. After this it was found that the fungi can incorporate many other chemicals into the side-chain. For example penicillin V has a phenoxyacyl group which is formed by adding phenoxyacetic acid to the medium.

It has been discovered that *Penicillium* produces small amounts of a compound which is a penicillin without an acyl group. This compound can be acylated chemically, making it possible to produce thousands of semi-synthetic penicillins, many of which have proved to be more efficient clinically than penicillin G. Furthermore, many bacteria produce an enzyme, penicillin amidase, which removes the acyl group from penicillin G. This enzyme is also used to convert penicillin G to more efficient semi-synthetic varieties.

● **Figure 3.8** Mycoprotein products.

Mycoprotein production

Quorn mycoprotein is a meat alternative produced by Marlow Foods (*figure 3.8*). It is made by growing a species of fungus, *Fusarium* ATCC 20334, in a continuous fermenter (*figure 3.9*). The main constituent of the medium used to grow *Fusarium* is glucose, made from hydrolysed starch. To this are added choline (a growth factor), ammonium phosphate, and small amounts of zinc, copper and iron sulphates. The medium is sterilised, and a starter culture of *Fusarium* is added. It is grown

under very carefully controlled conditions, including temperature, pH, nutrient concentrations, and dissolved oxygen. Ammonia gas is added to the fermenter to provide a nitrogen source for the fungus.

The *Fusarium* grows very quickly in the ideal conditions provided by the fermenter. The fungal hyphae are separated from the fermentation broth by centrifugation and the level of RNA is reduced using enzymes. The mycoprotein is then filtered, and steam is used to kill the fungus and wash it. The mycoprotein paste is mixed with a binder (egg white) and vegetable flavours to make a dough, which is then made into various products. Mycoprotein is grown using a continuous

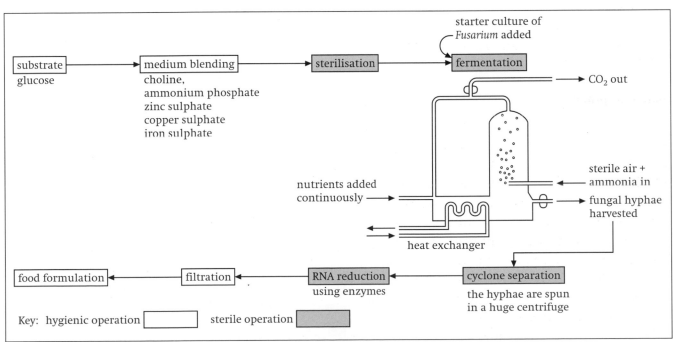

● **Figure 3.9** Flow chart for the production of mycoprotein.

process because this keeps the microorganism growing very rapidly. Since the microorganism is the product, this is very efficient.

SAQ 3.8

Suggest why the level of RNA is high in mycoprotein produced in this way.

SAQ 3.9

Name the carbon and nitrogen sources used in the production of   **a** penicillin;   **b** mycoprotein.

SAQ 3.10

Explain why penicillin production uses a batch process but mycoprotein uses a continuous process.

Investigating growth requirements

To investigate the effects of pH on the growth of a strain of *Bacillus*, a microbiologist would prepare a range of tubes containing buffered nutrient broth; for example at pH 3, 5, 6, 7 and 9. The tubes would have been sterilised by autoclaving and aseptic technique used to avoid contamination. Each tube would be inoculated with a loopful of broth culture of *Bacillus* and then incubated at 30 °C for 5–7 days. The cell density of each tube could then be measured using a spectrophotometer. A graph could then be plotted of cell density against pH to determine the most suitable pH for the culture of the *Bacillus*. This method can be used to investigate the growth requirements of a range of bacteria and fungi in liquid culture.

To investigate the effect of temperature on the growth rate of a fungus, such as *Fusarium*, aseptic technique would be used to inoculate several plates of potato dextrose agar (PDA) with a mycelial disc cut out of the edge of a fungal colony. This is best done with a heat-sterilised cork borer. The dishes would be inverted and incubated at a range of temperatures – for example, 5 °C (in the fridge), 20, 25, 30, 35 and 40 °C. It would be best to incubate several replicates at each temperature. At temperatures above 30 °C there is a tendency for the media to dry out, so it is suggested that a small dish of water is placed in the bottom of the incubator. The growth could be compared by measuring two diameters of each colony at right angles to each other, at 12-, 24- or 48-hour intervals, depending on the growth rate of the species. To determine the optimum temperature for the growth of *Fusarium*, a graph could be plotted of mean colony diameter against temperature of incubation.

SUMMARY

◆ Strict safety precautions are necessary when working with microorganisms. This is even more important in industrial and research laboratories where pathogenic or genetically engineered strains may be used.

◆ Fermenters and other equipment must be designed for aseptic operation, easy cleaning and sterilisation, and prevention of contamination and escape of organisms.

◆ There are two basic methods of culture: solid substrate and aqueous. Aqueous culture may be by the batch culture method, which is easier to operate, or by the more productive continuous culture method.

◆ Setting up an industrial process involves scaling up from laboratory scale to pilot plant scale, before finally growing the microorganism on industrial plant scale.

◆ Penicillin is an example of a product produced industrially by either a batch or fed-batch process.

◆ Mycoprotein is a meat substitute made by growing *Fusarium* fungus in a continuous fermenter.

Questions

1 Antibiotics are 'secondary metabolites'. What does this mean?

2 Do you think antibiotic production would be more efficient if a continuous fermentation system was used? Explain your answer.

3 Suggest techniques which might be used to extract antibiotics from the filtered medium.

4 In a test to find out whether a newly isolated organism **X** produces an antibiotic, the following procedure was carried out. First organism **X** was inoculated onto an agar plate, along the line **AB** (*figure 3.10*). Four different known species of bacteria were inoculated along **CD**, **EF**, **GH** and **IJ**. The plate was incubated for three days. What results would you expect to see if **X**:
   a has antibiotic activity,
   b does not have antibiotic activity?

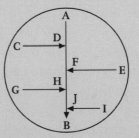

● **Figure 3.10** To find out if organism **X** produces an antibiotic.

5 Describe how a bulk fermenter is prepared for the fermentation process.

6 Manufacturers of antibiotics keep a pure stock culture of the microorganism to be used for the fermentation. This stock culture is used to produce a starter culture. What steps could be taken to ensure that the starter culture is pure?

7 Make a table to summarise the features of the different methods of fermentation and their relative advantages and disadvantages.

CHAPTER 4

Biotechnology in food production

By the end of this chapter you should be able to:

1 describe the production of novel genomes by the isolation of a gene from an organism, followed by its insertion into a new host organism;

2 describe the use of microorganisms as a food source, with reference to the production of mycoprotein and yeast extract;

3 describe and explain the role of biotechnology in the production of cheese, yogurt, beer and tenderised meat;

4 appreciate the potential social, economic, ethical and environmental implications of biotechnology and gene manipulation.

Genetic engineering

The **gene** is the basic unit of heredity: a piece of deoxyribonucleic acid (DNA) that codes for the production of a single protein. These proteins are usually enzymes, and because enzymes control the formation of many different substances, genes are able to exert a direct influence on the characteristics of an organism. A single gene which codes for a particular characteristic in this way can be passed on from generation to generation. (You may like to look back at *Biology 1*, chapter 5, to remind yourself about DNA and RNA.)

Genetic engineering or **modification** is a means of introducing new genes into cells or modifying existing genes. The resulting cells will, therefore, have new characteristics. Organisms which have been genetically engineered are often referred to as GMOs (genetically modified organisms).

In the early 1970s researchers found **restriction enzymes** in bacterial cells. These enzymes are part of the natural defence mechanism of bacteria and are released when any foreign nucleic acid enters the bacterial cell. For instance, when a virus invades a bacterium, it injects its own nucleic acid, either DNA or RNA, which 'reprogrammes'

the bacterial cells and uses the bacterial ribosomes to manufacture new virus particles. To defend itself, the bacterium produces restriction enzymes that cut the viral DNA or RNA into small fragments, which cannot reprogramme the cell. Genetic engineers have found these restriction enzymes useful for a number of reasons. Restriction enzymes are very specific and each recognises and cuts only one particular nucleotide sequence in the DNA.

Another useful property of restriction enzymes is that some of them have the ability to produce a staggered cut. This means that the fragments produced from a double strand of DNA have single-stranded 'sticky ends' protruding (*figure 4.1*). These single-stranded ends have a sequence of bases that can recognise and pair with one another. For example, the restriction enzyme *Eco*RI recognises the sequence GAATTC, and cuts the DNA between G and A so that the fragments have the sequence AATT on one end and TTAA on the other. The restriction enzyme *Hind*III recognises the sequence AAGCTT, and cuts the DNA between the two A bases so that AGCT is on one

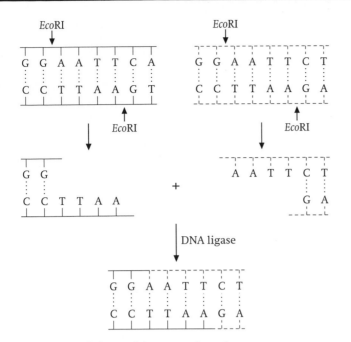

● **Figure 4.1** How 'sticky ends' are produced.

fragment and TCGA on the other. If the fragments are brought together, provided that the conditions are right, they will join together again and can be resealed by using another enzyme called a **DNA ligase**. This allows DNA from different sources to be combined, forming **recombinant DNA**. This will happen provided that the DNA fragments are cut originally by the same restriction enzyme.

SAQ 4.1

Find the restriction sites on the DNA sequence in *figure 4.2*, where *Eco*RI and *Hind*III would cut the DNA.

GGCATGAATCTATTAGCGAAGCTTCCCGGGATCTACTGGAATTCGCCGAAGCTTTC
CCGTACTTAGATAATCGCTTCGAAGGGCCCTAGATGACCTTAAGCGGCTTCGAAAG

● **Figure 4.2** DNA sequence.

Gene cloning

The reproduction of 'foreign' genes in bacterial or other cells is called **gene cloning**, a clone being a group of cells, organisms or genes that are exact copies of each other (*figure 4.3*). The 'foreign' gene has first to be inserted into the DNA of a culture of bacterial or other cells. The recombinant DNA is replicated as the cells divide and produces many copies of the gene.

Plasmids are circular strands of DNA which are found in many bacteria, and are separate from the bacterial chromosome. They are often used to insert foreign genes into cells. Viruses are also used.

When genetic engineering techniques are applied to microbial cells, not all the cells will contain recombinant DNA. It is important

that the genetic engineer can select out those cells which have been successfully **transformed** i.e. which contain the recombinant DNA. This is usually done by adding a '**marker gene**' as well as the gene that is required. These marker genes are often for antibiotic resistance, say tetracycline resistance. The genetic engineer can then select the transformed organisms by growing them on a medium containing tetracycline, so that all the untransformed bacteria will die.

Genetic engineering has revolutionised industrial processes. One advantage is that microorganisms can be genetically engineered to produce high yields, without the time-consuming process of mutation and selection. Sometimes the microorganism which synthesises a desired product is slow growing, so genetic engineers can insert the appropriate gene into the genome of a fast-growing organism, such as *E. coli* or *Saccharomyces cerevisiae*.

Recently, it has become possible to separate the growth phase from the production phase. The cells are allowed to grow and divide rapidly at first, without producing the required product. Once the correct cell density is reached, they can be genetically 'switched on' to produce the end-product by activating a key enzyme in the synthetic pathway. This is of particular use in fermentations where the end-product is toxic to the culture cells.

One problem with industrial-scale fermentations is that

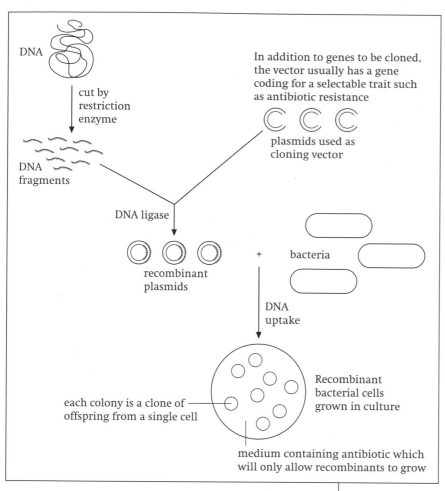

● **Figure 4.3** Gene cloning.

microorganisms produce a considerable amount of heat. Cooling the fermenter is expensive, so genetic engineers try to produce a thermophilic microorganism to synthesise the desired product.

SAQ 4.2

Why might bacteria from hot springs or thermal vents in the ocean be of interest to a genetic engineer?

Principles of biotechnology

Biotechnology is the application of biological systems, organisms or processes in manufacturing or service industries, such as genetic fingerprinting and gene therapy. It is a composite science, involving microbiology, genetics, biochemistry and engineering.

While biotechnology is a recent term, it is based on ancient technology. The brewing of beer appears to have begun in Babylon, before 6000 BC.

By about 3000 BC the Ancient Egyptians were brewing several kinds of beer including 'boozah', a type of acid beer produced by fermenting a dough made from germinated barley. Their skills were passed on via the Greeks to the Romans. In medieval times, some European monasteries were well-established breweries. The first recorded tax on beer in Britain was levied by Henry II in 1188. Distilled beverages, too, have an ancient origin. In 1000 BC, distilled beverages were made in China; whisky was being distilled in twelfth-century Ireland. Again, monasteries were particularly active in this field.

Breadmaking is another ancient technology. Remains of the Swiss lake settlers who lived 10 000 years ago show that they had developed the ability to make a kind of bread. From tombs in Ancient Egypt we can tell that the Egyptians had highly developed breadmaking skills (*figure 4.4*). They had made the discovery that if you left a piece of bread dough to stand for a few days before baking, its taste and structure improved. This was probably because of wild yeasts in the dough. The Egyptians developed the practice of keeping back a portion of the day's dough to inoculate the next day's bread or brew. By 100 BC, the Romans could buy bread in over 250 bread shops in the streets of Rome.

● **Figure 4.4** Models of breadmaking from an Ancient Egyptian tomb.

Cheese, wine, yogurt and vinegar have been made for centuries. More recently, in 1897, the Buchner brothers isolated enzymes from yeast, laying the foundations of enzyme technology. The discovery of antibiotics in 1929, and their large-scale production during the Second World War, created great advances in fermentation technology.

The latter half of the twentieth century saw great advances in biology. It has become the most diversified of the natural sciences. Since the 1950s there have been many technical advances, such as the electron microscope, and these have produced a proliferation of biological discoveries. In the last 20 years, more than 20 Nobel prizes have been awarded for discoveries in biotechnology and molecular biology. Perhaps the greatest contribution to modern biotechnology has been about 50 years' research into DNA. At the time, most of this research was thought to be of purely academic interest, but genetic manipulation is now a central theme in biotechnology. It is this which has transformed centuries of traditional technologies into modern industrial processes.

Already, the modern science of biology has made a great contribution to the quality of human life, but biotechnology promises far more than this. Modern biotechnology offers a variety of new industries, such as mining with microorganisms, new methods of fuel production, new pharmaceuticals, new ways of using industrial wastes and new food production techniques. It attempts to solve the greatest problems facing the modern world, such as the energy crisis, food shortage, pollution and disease. Biotechnological industries generally use cheap (often waste) substrates, operate at low temperatures and consume little energy. Microorganisms are often used that can be genetically manipulated. Since microorganisms are highly versatile, with rapid growth rates, the potential for new industries is enormous.

Biotechnology is an exciting and fast-growing area, offering enormous benefits and the prospect of solving many of the perplexing problems faced by the world today. However, like so many scientific advances, there is also the threat that these technologies could be used unethically, or that people's health and welfare might be harmed unless there are strict guidelines that are adhered to.

Biotechnology has an increasingly important role to play in agriculture. In the improvement of crop plants, for example, new strains of plants are being produced using genetic engineering techniques. The new plants may have an increased resistance to disease or pest attack or an enhanced capacity for nitrogen fixation. Genetic manipulation may improve the shelf-life of some plant products. The quality of plant products can also be improved, for example wheat proteins and high-yielding oilseed rape. Techniques have been developed to culture roots and shoots of certain plants that produce useful secondary metabolites in their cells, such as food colourings and flavourings (table 4.1). For example, mint shoot cultures are used to produce essential oils such as peppermint and spearmint.

In animals, biotechnology is used to make hormones which improve productivity. Bovine somatotrophin (BST) stimulates milk yields (page 57), and anabolic steroids may be used to increase muscle development. Genetic engineering techniques may be used to produce new breeds of animals with increased growth rates or milk yields.

Microorganisms can also be used to enhance agricultural production. An example is a silage inoculant called Ecosyl, developed by ICI. This contains a strain of the bacterium *Lactobacillus*

Product	Species	Application
quinine	*Cinchona officinale*	anti-malarial drug
ginger	*Zingiber officinale*	flavouring
codeine	*Papaver* spp.	analgesic (painkiller)
pyrethrins	*Chrysanthemum cinerarifolium*	insecticide
vincristine	*Catharanthus roseus*	anti-cancer drug
saffron	*Crocus sativus*	pigment, flavouring
digoxin	*Digitalis* spp. (foxglove)	heart drug
diosgenin	*Dioscorea deltoidea*	contraceptive
rose oil	*Rosa* spp.	perfume

● **Table 4.1** Some useful plant products.

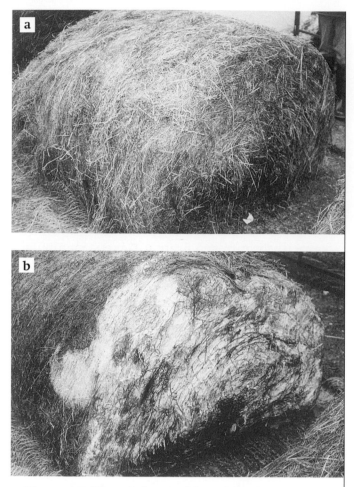

● **Figure 4.5** Silage bales **a** with and **b** without Ecobale additive.

plantarum. Silage is an animal feedstuff which is made from grass. Farmers harvest the grass and store it in silage pits or big polythene bales. Bacteria naturally present in the grass ferment the sugars in the grass to acids. These preserve the grass so that it can be fed to the animals throughout the winter when there is no fresh grass available.

However, silage made in this way is not always high quality as it depends on the nutrients in the grass and the microorganisms naturally present. Ecosyl is a fast-growing culture of lactic acid bacteria which compete well with the organisms naturally present. Farmers can apply the Ecosyl in powder form or spray it on to the harvested grass. The bacteria help the silage to ferment quickly to a stable pH. Tests show that the nutrient value of the silage is higher when fermented in this way. It is also more palatable and easier for cows to digest.

A similar silage inoculant, Ecobale, is made for farmers who make their silage in polythene bales. In addition to *Lactobacillus plantarum*, this inoculant also contains *Serratia rubidaea* and *Bacillus subtilis*. *L. plantarum* improves the quality of the silage, as already described, while *S. rubidaea* and *B. subtilis* inhibit the growth of moulds which can sometimes damage silage made in bales (*figure 4.5*).

Improving crop plants by genetic engineering

For centuries, plant breeders have improved the yields of major food crops such as wheat by selective breeding methods. In classical plant breeding the gene to be introduced must come from a plant that is fertile with the plant to be improved. So in wheat, for example, genetic variation can only be obtained from other wheat plants, or from very closely related ancestral grasses from which wheat has evolved. However, when wheat is crossed with these ancestral varieties, the embryos do not survive very well. New techniques have increased the rate of genetic exchange by promoting crossing-over during meiosis. This has led to the selection of embryos with genes from more distantly related plants because they are less likely to inherit harmful recessive genes from both parents.

Before genetic engineering techniques were used plant breeders induced mutations in selected plants by treating them with chemicals or radiation. This produces a greater range of variation in the offspring from which the better plants can be selected, but it is an unpredictable, lengthy and wasteful process. Now, modern molecular biology techniques involving gene insertion make possible the introduction of foreign genes from other species, whether they are distantly or closely related. Genetic engineering means that desirable genes can be selected, isolated and inserted into plants, which is a more accurate and less wasteful approach. Genes can be isolated from a whole range of organisms and then inserted into the plant using a gene-transfer vector such as a plasmid or virus. Any plant containing foreign genes is said to be **transformed**.

One widely used vector is the bacterium *Agrobacterium tumefaciens*. When this bacterium invades plant cells it causes a plant disease called

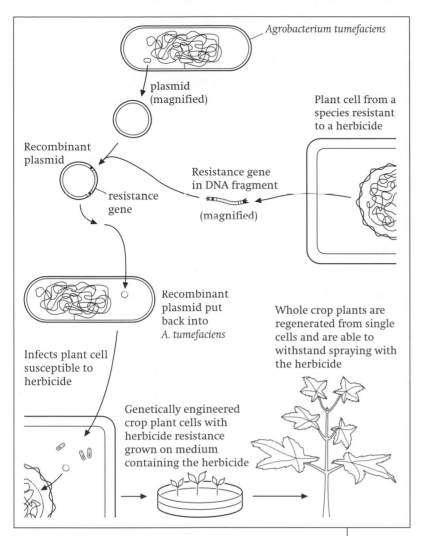

● **Figure 4.6** Transfer of resistance to a herbicide from a plant to a crop species.

crown gall, a form of cancerous growth. The bacterium has a large Ti (tumour-inducing) plasmid that becomes incorporated into the genome of the infected plant cell. Genetic engineers use restriction enzymes to insert the required gene into the Ti plasmid so that it can be introduced into the plant (*figure 4.6*). *Agrobacterium* has several strains so it is able to infect a wide range of plants.

At present, only single genes, or very small groups of genes, can be transferred. Examples of such characteristics are resistance to disease and to herbicides, such as glyphosate. Fields can be sprayed with the herbicide, but only the weed species die since the genetically engineered crop plants are resistant to it. The farmers have to spray fewer times as glyphosate is more effective than other weedkillers. This is less damaging to the environment.

Another example of genetic engineering in plants is the production of new varieties which emit a sky-blue glow when stressed. The amount of light emitted indicates the nature of the stress, such as drought, wind and exposure to frost. The bioluminescent protein aequorin occurs naturally in a species of blue jellyfish. Scientists have extracted the gene for this protein and have inserted it into some crop plants. The protein is sensitive to the level of calcium ions in plant cells, and stressed plant cells contain abnormally high levels of calcium ions. The protein undergoes a change to give the plant a coloured glow. Scientists hope that eventually these genetically engineered plants can be positioned among normal plants to act as living biosensors. (For more on biosensors, see pages 76–79.)

Breeding disease-resistant plants

Virus-resistant plants are also now being produced by gene transfer. *Agrobacterium* has been used to produce tomato and tobacco plants with increased resistance to the tobacco mosaic virus. *Agrobacterium* may also be used to improve resistance to the many fungal and bacterial diseases of plants by inserting genes which code for a substance toxic to the pathogen or for an enzyme which blocks an essential metabolic pathway.

SAQ 4.3
Suggest other qualities which could be genetically engineered into plants to create an improved strain.

Protoplast fusion is another technique used to transfer disease resistance in crop plants. Plant protoplasts can be produced by gently dissolving away the cellulose cell walls using cellulase and pectinase enzymes under carefully controlled iso-osmotic conditions with aseptic techniques. Protoplasts can then be fused together to form **heterokaryons**. Scientists have used this technique to transfer resistance to three major virus diseases from a naturally resistant wild variety of potato into commercial, high-yielding potato plants. Plant tissue culture techniques can then be used to grow new plants from hetero-karyons (see chapter 1).

Breeding insect-resistant plants

In Britain alone, millions of pounds a year are spent by farmers and growers in trying to control the tremendous amount of damage caused to crop plants by insect pests. However, insect pests are even more disastrous in some other countries. In parts of Africa locusts can completely destroy a whole field of crops in just a few hours. Particularly in the developed world, insecticides have been widely used to control insect pests but this has produced problems. One problem is that the first insecticides were broad spectrum, that is they were not only poisonous to the insect pests, but also to other insects and often to humans and other animals as well. The insecticides often destroyed the natural balance of organisms in the area; for example, they also killed predators of the pest so the population size of the pest would increase further and more insecticide would be needed. Some of these insecticides, such as DDT, do not break down easily and so accumulate in animals' bodies. Animals at the top of food chains could accumulate toxic levels of an insecticide. Furthermore, rain soon after spraying washes the insecticide off the plants and may pollute streams and rivers, killing plants and animals and damaging a greater area of the environment.

Recently, insecticides have been developed which are narrow spectrum, that is they only affect insects of one species or those most closely related. These cause less environmental damage and do not harm useful insects or other animals.

However, there are other ways to destroy insect pests which avoid the use of insecticides altogether. The bacterium *Bacillus thuringiensis* (often shortened to Bt) produces spores which contain a natural insecticide called the **T toxin**. If the spores are eaten by many kinds of leaf-eating caterpillars, or the larvae of flies and mosquitoes, the T toxin is broken down by digestive enzymes into toxic proteins. Only organisms with the correct enzymes are susceptible, so it is much more specific and thus safer to use than most insecticides. Useful insects, birds and most other wildlife are unaffected. There were problems though. *B. thuringiensis* does not survive well in the environment, so genetic engineers have had to clone bacteria carrying the appropriate gene which were more resistant. Many people who are concerned about releasing genetically engineered organisms into the environment find this unacceptable. So scientists have tried making an insecticide that contains T toxin by growing *B. thuringiensis*, drying it, and then applying the powder to the surface of plants. Unfortunately, this approach does not work very well as the T toxin is broken down within a few days. In addition, the T toxin is quite expensive to produce which makes it less economical to use.

Genetic engineers have attempted to solve these problems by engineering plants which carry the gene for the toxin. The T toxin gene has been inserted from *B. thuringiensis* into the Ti plasmid, and thereby into plants. The genetically engineered plants have been tested and have been found to be resistant to insect attack. Corn (maize) has been made resistant to the European corn borer in this way. Before the development of this genetically modified strain of corn, farmers in the USA, China, Brazil, Argentina, South Africa and Europe used to lose about 7% of their crop to this pest. Conventional crop protection agents have limited effectiveness against the corn borer. As soon as the larvae make their way into the plant's stalk, they cannot be reached by products sprayed on the plant. With the development of Bt corn, the problem has been solved. The Bt toxin gene has now been inserted into several kinds of crop plants, and it is hoped that it might lead to a reduction in the use of pesticides.

SAQ 4.4

Concern has been expressed recently about the release of genetically engineered strains of bacteria into the environment during trials for producing a natural insecticide. Describe the concerns which have been expressed and discuss their validity.

Genetically engineered farm animals

There are great possibilities for genetic engineering techniques in improving farm animals. One example is being developed in Australia to help control sheep tick. Ticks are external parasites which suck a sheep's blood. This can lead to severe secondary infections. At present tick infection is controlled by dipping the sheep in a chemical solution which kills the ticks on contact. Dipping has to be carried out regularly and is time-consuming. The dip can also be harmful to farm workers, who have to wear protective clothing and follow a rigorous set of safety procedures.

The outer covering of an insect, and the lining of its digestive system, contain chitin which can be broken down by chitinase. A chitinase gene occurs naturally in many plants. So far, scientists have successfully introduced the gene into mice. The next stage is to see whether the gene can be genetically engineered into sheep and whether the ticks will be affected by the chitinase produced in this way.

Bovine somatotrophin (BST)

Somatotrophin is a polypeptide normally secreted by the pituitary gland of mammals. It acts as a growth-stimulating hormone which increases the rate of protein synthesis, cell division and growth of bone. In cows, bovine somatotrophin increases milk production by diverting glucose, fatty acids and body fats to the mammary glands. Giving additional BST can increase these effects, for example the milk yield of a good dairy cow can be increased by up to 10 kg per day simply by injecting a small dose of BST into the cow every one or two weeks.

The BST for use in farming is produced by biotechnology. The gene for BST synthesis has been isolated from a cow and inserted into a plasmid from a bacterium. The plasmid is then used as a vector to insert the gene for BST synthesis into the bacterium *Escherichia coli*. The transfomed bacterium, containing the recombinant plasmid, is then allowed to multiply under carefully controlled conditions in a batch fermentation process. These cloned bacteria produce large quantities of BST as granules within their cells.

	feed in (kg day^{-1})	milk out (kg day^{-1})	milk to feed ratio
without BST	34.1	27.9	0.82
with BST	37.8	37.3	0.99

● **Table 4.2** Comparison of milk yields in a cow with and without BST treatment.

The bacteria are homogenised to split the cells open, releasing the granules along with cell debris. A very complex purification process then takes place, involving centrifugation and protein purification techniques to separate out the polypeptide BST from all the other cell proteins. The manufactured BST differs very slightly from natural BST because it has a few extra amino acids.

The highly purified BST is formulated into a slow-release preparation suitable for injection into cows. Very strict aseptic techniques must be applied throughout the manufacture and purification process.

Research has shown that BST increases lactation in cows but they need to eat more food (*table 4.2*).

Mastitis is a bacterial infection of the udder in milking cows. Cows with high milk yields are more likely to get mastitis, and recent studies have shown that cows given artificial BST are 79% more likely to become infected.

Apart from this, cows treated with artificial BST can conceive and give birth normally and their behaviour and temperament seem unaffected.

The United States Food and Drug Administration (FDA) approved the use of BST in the US in November 1993. Approval for the use of BST in the EU has not yet been granted, but there have been clinical trials.

There may be some drawbacks to its continued use. One concern is the possible risk to the consumer of drinking milk or eating meat which may have a higher than normal level of BST. The natural concentration in milk is usually around 2 parts per billion (ppb) but with treatment may be 10 ppb. BST should not be a risk to most consumers because it is a polypeptide and will be broken down to its constituent amino acids by the human digestive system. However, there is some concern about the effect of the hormone on pregnant and lactating mothers.

Other concerns are for the cows themselves. Prolonged use of BST has been shown to weaken the cow by depleting the immune system and producing an increased susceptibility to disease. Within the EU, there is already an over-production of milk. In the UK, milk quotas have been imposed on farmers to help control milk supply. So the use of BST does not have much to offer farmers except a small reduction in the size of their dairy herd, as farming costs could be reduced by getting the same quantity of milk from fewer cows. Alternatively, the use of BST may allow a more flexible management of milk supply. In August each year, there is a shortage of milk for cheese manufacture because autumn is a peak time for calving. BST could be given to help overcome this seasonal shortfall, rather than as a way of increasing milk supply overall.

SAQ 4.5 _____
Summarise the advantages and disadvantages of using BST.

SAQ 4.6 _____
Why are aseptic techniques used in the manufacture of BST?

Single cell protein (SCP)

Microorganisms can be grown on a whole range of cheap or waste materials, harvested and then purified or processed to provide food for either humans or livestock. If the foodstuff produced is a protein, the product is called single cell protein (SCP). Many microorganisms are suitable for this process, including algae, blue-greens, fungi and bacteria.

Examples of substrates available
- The cheese industry produces large amounts of whey, much of which is wasted. Whey contains both protein and lactose, and some yeasts can grow on this waste to produce high-grade protein and certain vitamins. The product is used to supplement cattle feed.
- The sugar refining industry produces molasses.

At present, some of this waste is fermented and distilled to produce rum and some is fed directly to cattle. However, yeast can be grown on molasses to give very high yields of cattle feed.
- Sulphite liquor is a waste product from the wood pulping industry and contains low levels of sugar. Fungi can grow on this.
- The oil industry burns off considerable quantities of natural gas while producing oil because it is uneconomic to use the gas. In the future it could become economic to liquefy and store the gas for conversion to methanol, which would support bacteria and yield high-value protein.
- In oil distillation, straight-chain alkanes are produced as a rather waxy waste product. They are of limited use in other industries, but they can be used as a substrate for yeasts which can then become animal feed.

Advantages of using microorganisms to produce SCP
- Microorganisms have very rapid growth rates. If conditions for growth are kept at an optimum, some microorganisms can double their biomass every 20 minutes.
- Microorganisms can exploit a great variety of substrates, particularly wastes and other substances of low commercial value.
- The genetic characteristics of microorganisms can be manipulated fairly easily and they can readily be screened for desirable characteristics such as high growth rate or lipid content.
- Microorganisms have a fairly high protein content with a good proportion of essential amino acids.
- Many foodstuffs and secondary plant products can only be grown in warm climates, but with fermenters they can be produced almost anywhere. Fermenters also require very little land area.

Problems encountered with SCP
SCP is often contaminated with the substrate, as total purification is not feasible. This creates a problem where the substrate is toxic, such as sewage or methanol. This problem can be over-come by adding an extra stage in the food chain.

For example the toxic substrate is used to grow organism A. Organism A is then used as a substrate for organism B, which is then harvested to yield SCP.

This is safer, but as the food chain is longer, the process is less efficient due to energy losses at each trophic level. Alternatively, a product may be produced from the toxic waste and then used as a substrate for SCP. An example of this is when sewage is converted to methane by methanogenic bacteria. The methane is then used as the substrate on which to grow single-cell protein.

Another problem is that prokaryotic micro-organisms used for SCP production have a high nucleic acid content (page 47). This happens particularly where production is by continuous fermentation, since growth is exponential. Nucleic acid content is about 15% of the dry mass of bacteria, but only about 4% in meat and fish. Excess nucleic acid in human diets leads to health problems, such as kidney stones, and can cause nausea, vomiting and diarrhoea. Using chemical methods or enzymes to reduce nucleic acid levels is prohibitively expensive, so prokaryotic SCP is best used either as a human food supplement or for feeding farm animals. Eukaryotic SCP, based on algae and fungi, does not give such problems as the nucleic acid content is much lower.

Scientists must also choose the species of microorganism carefully, so that there is no risk of pathogens being present. *Pseudomonas* is a useful bacterium which grows on various hydro-carbons and methanol. However, some related species of *Pseudomonas* are pathogens and scientists are concerned that if the organism undergoes a genetic change it could cause disease. One way to avoid this is to kill the microorganism during some stage of SCP processing.

Using microorganisms as food

As described in chapter 3, Marlow foods make a meat substitute called Quorn mycoprotein by growing *Fusarium*, a filamentous fungus, on waste starch in a continuous fermenter.

Spirulina is a blue-green bacterium which has been grown for many years as food. Because it is photosynthetic, it grows in ponds, needing only carbon dioxide and inorganic ions. Dried *Spirulina* has a high nutrient value and can be fed to animals. It is also gaining popularity as a health food.

ICI used to make a single cell protein, Pruteen, which was used as an animal feed. Work started in the early 1970s when they found a very tiny rod-shaped bacterium, *Methylophilus methylotrophus*, which would grow very efficiently using methanol and ammonia as a substrate. In 1972 a pilot plant was set up, and in 1979 an enormous pressure cycle fermenter went into production. Unfortunately, the process did not prove to be economic as other forms of animal feed, such as fish-meal, were cheaper. As a result, the Pruteen plant was closed down in the mid-1980s.

SAQ 4.7

Why are widely available, cheap, waste products used as substrates for single cell protein production?

Yeast extract

Breweries produce large amounts of yeast (page 62), and while some of it is used to inoculate the next brew, not all is required. Some of the yeast is filtered off and sold to whisky distilleries. Malt whisky is made in a similar way to beer, by ferment-ing a mash made from malted barley. However, to produce the whisky the fermented malt is boiled and the whisky distilled off. This process kills all the yeast in the brew, so the distiller has no left-over yeast to inoculate the next brew and needs a steady supply of fresh brewers' yeast.

Dried yeast is a rich source of water-soluble vitamins, including all the B-complex vitamins. It is a particularly rich source of the vitamins riboflavin and niacin, and is often sold in tablet form.

Spent brewers' yeast is also used to make other foods. During the nineteenth century, the German chemist Liebig became interested in the use of waste brewery yeast. He knew it was nutritious, and studied the problem of converting it to a palatable food product. Eventually he realised that, if he left the yeast to undergo a period of self-digestion and then concentrated it, he could make a product suitable for human consumption. Self-digestion of the yeast is called **autolysis**, and in this process the enzymes present in the yeast cell itself are used to break down the proteins, nucleic acids, carbohydrates and so on. The process discovered by Liebig occurs naturally, but it happens more quickly when the yeast is heated to 50 °C and salt is added. It normally takes about a day for most of the proteins to be broken down into amino acids, then the mixture is filtered and concentrated into a thick paste. One type of yeast extract manufactured in this way is marketed as Marmite.

Large quantities of fresh yeast arrive daily at the Marmite factory, and are subjected to autolysis in large tanks and copper vats. The liquid cell contents, called the **autolysate**, are separated from the cell walls by centrifugation and filtration. The residual cell walls are used for animal feed. Water is evaporated from the liquid autolysate in vacuum condensers to give a suitable consistency. It is carefully examined in the laboratories, then blended and flavoured with vegetable extracts before being packed in sterilised glass containers.

Yeast hydrolysates are made by boiling the yeast with hydrochloric acid, which hydrolyses most of the proteins to amino acids. It is then neutralised with sodium hydroxide, filtered, and concentrated into a thick paste. The final product tastes salty because of the salt produced by neutralisation of the acid.

Both autolysates and hydrolysates have a meaty flavour and are used as additives to food products where a meaty flavour is required, such as in soups and sauces, frozen foods, stews, hamburgers, sausages, gravies and to flavour snack products such as potato crisps. The meaty flavour of yeast autolysates is probably due to the large number of amino acids and small peptides it contains, but its flavour enhancement properties are probably due to nucleotides.

Cheese

Cheese has been made since ancient times, when it was an important method of preserving food. Today, every part of the world has its own characteristic cheeses, depending on the starter culture of bacteria and the type of milk.

The first stage in cheese making is **ripening of the milk**. This means that the milk is heated, and a starter culture of bacteria is added to speed up the natural process of milk souring. The starter culture is made up of lactic acid bacteria, such as *Streptococcus lactis*, *S. cremoris* and *S. lactis* subsp. *diacetylactis*. As the milk ripens, lactic acid is produced. When the pH has fallen to the desired level, the milk is kept warm and rennet is added. Rennet is an enzyme, found naturally in the stomachs of young mammals, which **coagulates** milk. When the milk has set adequately, the solid curd is chopped up using special knives, releasing a lot of the liquid whey which is trapped inside the curd. The curd is continuously stirred, and at the same time it is **scalded** or heated to release more of the whey. During this stage, temperature and pH must be carefully controlled to maintain cheese quality and to avoid destroying the starter bacteria. After this, stirring is stopped so that the curd settles. The **whey** is drained off and the curd chopped up to release more whey. Next, the curd is **milled** and **salted**. An electric mill is used to cut the blocks of curd into smaller pieces, then salt is added as a preservative and flavour enhancer. To make a hard cheese, such as cheddar, the salted curd is filled into moulds or hoops and pressed.

The cheese is then left to **ripen** or **mature**. The cheese is placed in a ripening room at a controlled temperature and humidity. During this stage, bacterial and enzymatic changes occur which give the cheese its characteristic flavour. During ripening most of the lactic acid streptococci are inhibited, but lactobacilli and others proliferate. All the lactose is converted to lactic and other organic acids. Proteins are converted to peptones and amino acids. Enzymes convert some of the fats to fatty acids and glycerol. Amines, aldehydes and ketones are also produced, adding to the cheese flavour. The finished cheese contains approximately 0.1% microorganisms by weight, that is, about 10^8 microorganisms per gram.

Blue cheeses, such as Danish Blue, Roquefort and blue Stilton, all have blue veins due to the mould *Penicillium roquefortii*. The cheese is pierced with stainless steel skewers, which allow air to penetrate and enable the mould to grow faster. The blue colour is due to spore production by the mould. The mould produces enzymes, which hydrolyse fats into fatty acids and ketones, adding to the flavour of the cheese. Many blue cheeses have a wrinkled outer drying coat, which supports the growth of many microorganisms, such as moulds, yeasts, streptococci and lactobacilli.

Soft cheeses, such as cottage cheese, are unripened and unpressed. This means they have a much higher water content than hard cheeses. The whey is drained off slowly using gravity, and no pressure is applied.

SAQ 4.8

Cheese making is basically the same for all kinds of cheese, yet there is an enormous variety of cheeses on sale in the shops. Which stages in cheese making might be the source of these differences?

Yogurt

Yogurt has been made for thousands of years in eastern Europe and western Asia. Traditional yogurt was much thinner and more acidic than the yogurt now readily available in shops and supermarkets which has been developed to suit modern tastes.

Yogurt is made by fermenting milk with a carefully cultured mixture of microorganisms. Whole, semi-skimmed or skimmed milk may be used. Sugar and/or starch may be added for certain products. The milk must first be tested to check for contamination by pathogenic bacteria due to lack of hygiene during milking and also to check for antibiotics that might have been used to treat infections in cows. Then it is processed and a starter culture of bacteria is added to begin the fermentation. Commercial yogurt is usually made from concentrated skimmed milk. The milk may have been homogenised to make the mixture smoother and thicker and to lessen the risk of separation during incubation and processing.

The milk is heated to between 85 °C and 95 °C for 15–30 minutes. This has several effects including killing most of the bacteria in the milk, making it easier for the starter microorganisms to establish themselves. In addition the milk whey proteins are denatured so they can interact with the milk protein casein to produce a thicker texture. Most of the dissolved air is removed, improving the conditions for growth of the

microaerophilic organisms (those that grow best at low oxygen levels) in the culture. The milk is then cooled to just below 45 °C, which is the optimum temperature for the growth of lactobacilli in the starter culture.

At this point the starter culture is added and the milk is incubated at 38–44 °C for 4 to 6 hours or at 32 °C for 12 hours. The starter culture usually consists of a mixture of *Lactobacillus bulgaricus* and *Streptococcus thermophilus* which grow in symbiosis, that is they each produce conditions which encourage growth in the other species. Lactobacilli break down protein to release peptides, which encourage the growth of the streptococci. When growing vigorously, the streptococci produce methanoic acid which stimulates the growth of the lactobacilli. At the end of the incubation period, the pH has fallen to around 4.4. During the incubation *L. bulgaricus* also produces lactic acid. Both microorganisms produce ethanal which gives the yogurt its characteristic flavour. Fruit, nuts or flavours may be added to the finished yogurt, having first been sterilised to prevent contamination by yeasts and other bacteria. After incubation, the thickened yogurt is cooled to 4.5 °C and held at this temperature for packing. When packed the yogurt is stored at 2 °C. The bacteria remain alive but are inactive at this temperature.

Recently, so-called 'bio' yogurts have become very popular. These produce a creamier tasting, sweeter yogurt. The starter culture for bio yogurts contains *S. thermophilus* and *L. bulgaricus* as before, but also contains *L. acidophilus* and *Bifidobacterium bifidum*.

SAQ 4.9

How might milk become contaminated with antibiotics? Why must the milk used in yogurt manufacture be free from all traces of antibiotic?

SAQ 4.10

Why must the milk mixture be cooled before the starter culture is added?

SAQ 4.11

Why does the pH fall during the incubation?

SAQ 4.12

Why is it not necessary to kill the bacteria before eating the yogurt?

SAQ 4.13

The yogurt vats and pipework in the factory must be sterilised between each batch. Why is this necessary and how might it be done?

Beer

Beer is made from malted barley (*figure 4.7*). To malt the barley the grains are soaked in water for 2–3 days, drained and then incubated at 13–17 °C for 10 days. This causes the grain to germinate, producing amylase enzymes, which convert the stored starch to maltose. The temperature is then raised to 40–70 °C to stop germination by denaturing enzymes. Malting is often carried out by specialist maltsters and the malt sent to the brewery. There are different types of malt, depending on the roasting temperatures used, and these impart different colours and flavours to the brew. Generally, lager malts are roasted at a lower temperature than beer malts.

The roasted grains are cracked open by passing between rollers. The crushed malt is called **grist**. This is mixed with hot brewing water at 62–68 °C in a large vessel to produce a **mash**. The mash stands for about two hours to allow the sugars to be dissolved out of the malt. It then passes into another large vessel where sugary liquid called wort is drained off. The grain is sprayed with hot water to wash the sugars out of the grains, which act as a filter. The spent grain is left behind and sold for cattle fodder.

Hops are added to give the characteristic bitter flavour of beer. Traditional breweries add dried hops in 'leaf' form, but modern breweries use hops which have been pressed into pellets, which reduces their transport and storage costs. A small amount of sugar is also added. Large copper vats are used to boil the wort for several hours to concentrate it. The boiled wort is separated from the spent hops which are sold for hop manure. The wort is then passed through heat exchangers to cool it to a suitable temperature for fermentation.

Yeast is added to the cooled wort in the fermenting vessel. *Saccharomyces cerevisiae* is used for beer and *S. carlsbergensis* for lager. Traditionally, lager yeasts grow at the bottom of the vessel and are called 'bottom fermenters' whereas beer yeasts grow on the surface of the wort and are known as 'top fermenters'. The newer varieties of beer yeasts are bottom fermenters, enabling breweries to use the same type of fermenter for either process. Initially, there is a fairly high oxygen content in the wort, and breweries may even aerate the brew,

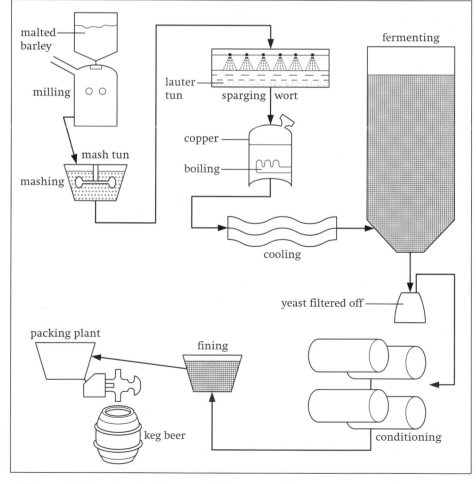

● **Figure 4.7** Summary diagram of beer manufacture.

encouraging the yeast to divide rapidly so as to increase the numbers present. After this, conditions become anaerobic and fermentation begins. The yeast converts the sugars to ethanol and carbon dioxide in 2–5 days, after which the yeast is separated off. Some is used to inoculate the next batch and the rest is sold for products such as yeast extract (Marmite) (see page 59). Sometimes the carbon dioxide is collected and sold.

Traditional beers are stored in barrels. Modern beers are filtered, pasteurised, standardised (brought to a standard colour and flavour) and canned or bottled.

Recently, there have been developments to produce both wine and beer by continuous fermentation methods. In these processes, the yeast is kept in its exponential growth phase so that the product is made much more quickly. This process is particularly popular for making lager, which can be made in about four hours instead of several days. However, although this process is more economical, the flavour and alcohol content are reduced.

SAQ 4.14
What is the difference between a 'top-fermenting' and a 'bottom-fermenting' yeast?

SAQ 4.15
Explain why beer produced by continuous fermentation would have a lower alcohol content than its traditionally produced equivalent.

Enzymes and meat tenderisation

Enzymes can be used in meat tenderisation, either naturally or artificially. Animal carcasses used for meat are usually kept in cold storage for 10–12 days after slaughter. During this time, the lysosomes within the cells burst open and release proteases, which bring about autolysis of the tissues. These enzymes catalyse the breakdown of fibrous proteins such as collagen and elastin which hold the connective tissue together. This process releases the bundles of muscle fibres and therefore increases the tenderness of the meat.

In some countries, but not yet in the UK, a protease may be injected into the bloodstream of cattle just before slaughter, or added just after slaughter. One such enzyme, known as **papain**, is extracted from the sap of the papaya plant, *Caryca papaya*. Papain is sold commercially for application to meat in the home prior to cooking. However, most meat is tenderised during the cooking process before the proteases are denatured at around 90 °C and papain is really only useful for the cheaper cuts.

SAQ 4.16
What are the arguments for and against the injection of a protease into cattle immediately prior to slaughter?

Implications of genetic engineering

The law and patents
Biotechnological advances have created many legal issues. Lawyers work very differently from scientists, by examining facts in the light of existing laws, which means that new developments may take months or years to become accepted. One of the most important areas is in patent law. A **patent** is the exclusive right to manufacture or use an invention. When a scientist invents a new process or product, the scientist or the company he or she works for does not have the automatic right to the invention, unless the scientist or company applies for, and is granted, a patent. If a patent is not secured, then other scientists and companies are entitled to benefit from the invention. There are many difficulties in obtaining a patent. If the lawyers decide that the invention is not sufficiently different from other patented inventions, then a new patent is not granted. Something like a new antibiotic, or a new microorganism that could degrade a toxin previously resistant to breakdown, might well be granted a patent. When filing a patent, a fairly detailed description of the invention must be supplied which is then available for public inspection. Companies sometimes feel that publishing a patent will aid their competitors, so decide

against filing a patent and keep it a trade secret instead. In 1987 the US Patent Office announced that life forms other than microorganisms could be patented, and in 1988 the first patent for a genetically engineered animal, a transgenic mouse useful in cancer research, was granted.

SAQ 4.17

Summarise briefly, in your own words, what a patent is, and explain why companies may not always obtain a patent for a new product they develop.

The dangers of release

Genetically engineered microorganisms are widely used in fermentation processes to make pharmaceutical and other products. Concern has been expressed about the possible dangers to workers if these organisms are accidentally released. However, these fears are decreasing since the fermentation plants can be made virtually leak-proof, and the microorganisms are killed at the end of the process. Furthermore, genetically engineered strains of *E. coli* and yeast, the two most common organisms, are not capable of inhabiting the human gut. Greater concerns are expressed about genetically engineered microorganisms which might be deliberately released into the environment. One example is the use of microorganisms to prevent frost damage to plants. Frost-sensitive plants cannot tolerate ice crystal formation within their tissues, since water expands on freezing and destroys the cell structure. Certain bacterial species which are found naturally on the surface of plants, such as *Pseudomonas syringae* and *Erwinia herbicola*, contain an ice nucleation gene which initiates ice formation at temperatures of 1.5–5 °C, probably because of a protein in the membrane. The gene for ice nucleation has been cloned and is being investigated. A strain of *P. syringae* which lacks the ice nucleation gene has been developed. If legal restrictions can be overcome, this might be sprayed on potato plants to compete with bacteria already there which possess the ice nucleation gene, and so reduce frost damage. The unmodified

bacteria are currently being used to form 'artificial' snow on ski slopes: water containing *P. syringae* is sprayed through a fine nozzle onto a fan, and the resultant cooling produces snow.

Sometimes cultures of microorganisms are sent through the post, and concern has been expressed that dangerous or genetically modified microorganisms might be accidentally released from a badly packed parcel. The greatest fear concerned with releasing these microorganisms is that they may proliferate in the environment. If some previously unknown hazard was discovered after the organism had been released, then there is no way that all the genetically engineered microorganisms could be destroyed. Scientists have attempted to introduce a so-called 'suicide' gene into organisms intended for release, but this is not fool-proof, since natural selection would favour any mutants which lacked the gene. However, farmers have been adding nitrogen-fixing bacterial cultures to the soil for many years now, with no detrimental effects on the environment. It is unlikely that a well-studied organism, with only two or three readily identified genes added, could become a hazard. Even so, the concerns about mutation, and hybridisation with natural microorganisms, are thought by many scientists to be largely unfounded, since exchange of genetic material occurs all the time in natural bacterial populations.

Unseen consequences

Some people are concerned that we do not know the consequences of transferring genes from one organism to another, and feel this is unnatural. However, genetic engineers argue that we have been introducing new genes to organisms for the last 50 years, using conventional breeding programmes. This experience leads them to believe that introduced genes do not behave differently from the organism's own genes. However, we still need to research how stable genetically modified organisms will be in the long term, and to find out about the effects of introducing several 'foreign' genes to an organism. There are fears that inserting 'new' genes might activate harmful genes that are already present but not being expressed. For example, inserting a gene into a crop plant might activate a toxin gene, causing the plant to produce a harmful toxin as well as the novel product. However, highly purified materials obtained from genetically modified crops are identical to those from non-modified crops. For example, sucrose made from a genetically engineered strain of sugar cane which is resistant to insect attack is identical to normal sucrose.

Some crop plants that are normally used for food, e.g. oilseed rape, are currently being developed as 'bioreactors' to manufacture pharmaceutical products or chemicals to make biodegradable plastics. Some food plants, such as bananas, are being used to produce vaccines. There are fears that, unless these plants are kept well-segregated from normal food crops, genes could inadvertently enter the food chain by cross-pollination, or crops could be accidentally mixed during harvesting.

One concern about herbicide-resistant crops is that this will lead to the more effective destruction of weeds. This, in turn, will reduce the availability of habitats for insects and other invertebrates, and this could have implications for the whole ecosystem. There are also fears that the herbicide-resistance gene could spread to weed species by cross-pollination. A further problem is that genetically modified seed is produced by a few major pharmaceutical companies, who also manufacture the weedkiller, and can make enormous profits. Some people are concerned that farmers in developed countries will produce greater yields and profits by using genetically engineered seed, while farmers in developing countries will not be able to afford the seed and will become even more disadvantaged.

Antibiotic resistance genes

Antibiotic resistance genes are often used as 'marker genes' when organisms are being genetically engineered, for example when transferring a new gene into a crop plant (see page 51). These marker genes make it easier to select the modified cells in the laboratory. There are fears that these antibiotic resistance genes may be transferred to bacteria present in the gut of the consumer. If the antibiotic resistance gene passed to bacteria which cause human disease, then these bacteria would be resistant to the antibiotics that would normally

be prescribed to kill them. It is very unlikely that antibiotic resistance could be spread in this way, since the processing of food usually causes the DNA to be degraded. However, it is possible (though time-consuming) to remove these marker genes later, or to use alternative marker genes.

There are two main concerns about genetically engineered plants. Firstly, such qualities as increased photosynthetic efficiency and herbicide resistance could possibly transfer into weed species through hybridisation, resulting in 'super-weeds'. However, traditional plant breeding methods already achieve crop plants with advantageous genetic qualities which could result in this problem. The difference with genetic engineering is simply that the process is quicker. Secondly, the cloning vectors used in genetic engineering are relatives of plant pathogens. There is concern that this could result in disease transmission, should the inserted viral DNA separate from the host cell DNA. It is extremely unlikely that genetically engineered crop plants present a hazard to the environment, but nevertheless, there are strict laws in many countries about the release and use of genetically modified organisms (GMOs).

Genetically engineered herbicide-resistant plants also pose another problem. Many people feel that the development of these plants will lead to an increase in the use of herbicides, which are considered to be environmentally undesirable. The companies which are developing these plants claim that they hope to increase their market share, rather than increasing total herbicide use, by means of these plants. Farmers will use a specific, environmentally friendly herbicide when growing these plants, and the companies claim this will lead to an overall decrease in herbicide use.

Preventing gene transfer

There are several ways of introducing new genes into organisms in such a way as to minimise the chance of transferring them to other organisms. Sometimes a new gene can be inserted into the chloroplasts and, as most plants do not transfer chloroplasts by pollen, this would prevent the new gene being spread by cross-pollination. Another approach is to link the inserted gene to a gene which switches off pollen production, so that the plant is sterile. A third approach is called 'terminator technology'. This is a technique which stops the seed of genetically engineered crop varieties from germinating. This would mean that farmers have to buy new seed each year. Concerns have been expressed that farmers would be unable to store some of their harvested seed for future use, which would be a particular worry for farmers in developing countries. However, several major biotechnology companies have now agreed to stop developing 'terminator technology' so that farmers would be able to save and store seed if they wish.

It is important that genetically engineered crops are grown at a suitable isolation distance from other crops of related species, so that cross-pollination is unlikely. However, it is impossible to keep a crop totally isolated. For example, seeds and pollen from genetically engineered crops may be spread by birds or animals.

SAQ 4.18

What type of gene do you think a so-called 'terminator gene' might be?

Competition with natural species

Another concern is that a genetically engineered microorganism may compete with the natural species in a habitat and ultimately lead to the loss of the natural species. This has been seen in the introduction of animals and plants to different countries, where their spread has sometimes been uncontrollable, for example the rabbit in Australia. Clearly an assessment of potential risk to the environment must be made before any genetically engineered organism is released, but there is dispute about designing a relevant test.

New drugs

In the next decade, many more new drugs, such as viral vaccines and human proteins, will become available as a result of developments in recombinant DNA technology. However, since the quality of the drug rather than its mode of production is important, it appears likely that these drugs will probably not be regulated any differently from conventionally produced drugs. Indeed, many of these drugs may be safer: human growth hormone used to be produced from corpses, with the risk of transmitting Creutzfeld–Jacob disease (see page 74).

Slightly more concern surrounds domestic animals. If the animal is to be used as a source of human food, it is important that the drug does not contaminate the slaughtered animal. Bovine somatotrophin (BST) can increase milk production by 10–25% when administered to cows (page 57). Scientists in the US Food and Drug Administration have decided that the use of BST in dairy cattle presents no health risk to consumers, yet in both Europe and the USA there has been a great deal of anxiety about its use.

Gene therapy

A sample of cells can be taken from the blood or bone marrow of a patient, treated by genetic manipulation, and then replaced. One of the fears of scientists working in this field of somatic (body) cell gene therapy is that some cells harbour viruses that might act as helpers and enable the vector to spread. Also the insertion of new DNA sequences into chromosomes might activate **oncogenes**, latent genes associated with cancer. Ultimately, genetic engineering may be applied to the DNA of the cells themselves in order to treat inherited diseases. Somatic cells are non-reproductive cells, so any genetic changes produced in these cells will not be passed on to the patient's children. Only diseases caused by mutation in single genes could be treated by somatic cell gene therapy; diseases due to whole chromosome defects are technically too difficult to treat.

The risks and benefits of genetic engineering on germ-line (reproductive) cells are still not clear. There are also many ethical considerations. Before considering any treatment, scientists would have to reduce the risk of a misplaced piece of DNA triggering cancer genes. The chances of interfering with an essential gene function are much higher in germ-line therapy. For example, damage to a gene coding for an essential brain function would not affect the viability of bone marrow cells or blood cells, but it would certainly affect an embryo.

There is also the risk that, in the future, germ-line techniques could be used for **eugenics**, that is to breed humans selectively. It may be possible in the near future, when more is known of the human genome sequence, to tell from a person's genes exactly what characteristics they will inherit. If gene therapy is sufficiently advanced by then, scientists may be able to alter characteristics and correct 'defects'. For some inherited diseases, such gene therapy would be beneficial. However, there may be the temptation to produce a clone of 'super-people' selected for high intelligence or super fitness.

Economic benefits

Biotechnology has certainly brought economic benefits, but mainly to richer countries. An example of this is high fructose corn syrup (HFCS). HFCS is produced from corn (maize) starch by enzyme conversion, firstly by hydrolysing the starch into glucose, and then by converting the glucose to fructose, which is one-and-a-half times sweeter than table sugar (sucrose). This is widely used in the USA, although tariffs levied under the European Common Agricultural Policy mean that it is very expensive in Europe. However, another biotechnologically produced artificial sweetener is aspartame, a dipeptide which has virtually no calories and is nearly 200 times sweeter than table sugar. This is greatly in demand as a sweetener, particularly in soft drinks. These sweeteners have greatly reduced the sugar imports into countries like the USA, and the reduced demand has caused the world price of sugar to fall disastrously, threatening the livelihoods of many farmers in countries like the Philippines.

Biotechnology has also improved yields of certain crops. As you read in chapter 1, the addition of cyanobacteria (blue-greens) to paddy fields greatly enhances rice production, because of

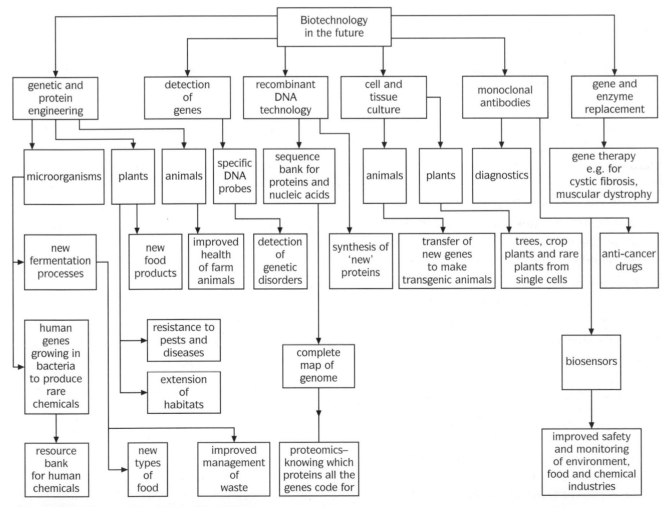

● **Figure 4.8** The future of biotechnology.

the nitrates produced by the cyanobacteria. This means that countries like India and Indonesia no longer need to import rice, destroying the livelihoods of many farmers in rice-producing countries like Thailand and Pakistan.

There have been many economic benefits to wealthier countries, where biotechnology has created skilled employment and improved quality of life in many areas such as health care. However, even agriculture may be threatened in these countries. More efficient, genetically engineered crop plants and farm animals treated with growth hormones will mean that more food can be produced in a smaller area. Healthy meat substitutes, such as mycoprotein, may reduce the demand for meat. In the future, agricultural crops may be used for a variety of purposes rather than just one. At present, grain crops are used only for food and animal feed, but they could become a source of starch for various industries and cellulose for making textiles and paper. Already, researchers at the Carlsberg company in Denmark are developing this concept. All these changes mean that smaller, less efficient farmers may go out of business.

Ethical implications

Many people feel that it is morally wrong to genetically engineer animals purely for human benefit. This argument is used particularly when genetically engineered animals are designed to suffer, such as the transgenic mouse which was developed at Harvard for cancer research. Some people feel that any food products made from genetically engineered plants or animals should be specially labelled, so that customers have the choice of whether to buy them or not.

The possible future of biotechnology is summarised in *figure 4.8* on page 67.

SUMMARY

◆ Genetic engineering involves the insertion of new genes into plant, animal, fungal or microbial cells to produce an organism with novel characteristics.

◆ Biotechnology has an important role in agriculture; microorganisms can be used as silage inoculants; crop plants may be genetically engineered to become resistant to diseases, insects or herbicides; farm animals may be genetically engineered to have desirable properties, or they may be treated with hormones to give increased productivity.

◆ Microorganisms can produce single cell protein from waste substrates, which can then be used as a human or animal foodstuff.

◆ Cheese and yogurt are made from milk by the action of selected bacteria.

◆ Yeast is used in the production of beer. By-products, such as spent brewers' yeast, can be used in products such as yeast extract.

◆ Enzymes are used in many ways to enhance food production, for example in meat tenderisation.

◆ There is public concern about genetically engineered plants, animals and micro-organisms, and whether they pose any risk when released into the environment. Genetic engineering could lead to improvements in agriculture, but there is concern that there could be serious environmental and economic consequences.

Questions

1 Fungi can be used to make meat substitutes for human consumption, such as Quorn. What structural features of fungi make them particularly suitable for this purpose?

2 Write an essay on ways in which biotechnology might help to overcome the problem of world food shortage.

3 Look at some food packets in your house, such as crisps, soups, gravy powders and sauce mixes. See if they use yeast hydrolysates or autolysates.

4 One strand of the base sequence in DNA recognised by the restriction enzyme *Eco*RI is shown in *figure 4.9*.

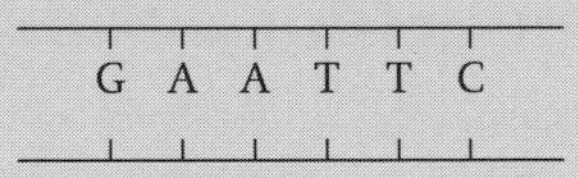

G   A   A   T   T   C

● **Figure 4.9**

a Write in the base sequence found on the complementary strand.

b *Eco*RI cuts the sugar phosphate 'backbones' between guanine and adenine nucleotides whenever it recognises the sequence –GAATTC. Draw base sequence diagrams to show the sticky ends produced by the action of this enzyme.

Figure 4.10 is a map of a plasmid showing the positions of the recognition sequences of three restriction enzymes, *Pst*I, *Eco*RI and *Hind*III. The shaded areas represent two genes, one for resistance to the antibiotic tetracycline and the other for resistance to the antibiotic ampicillin. Pieces of human DNA obtained by cutting with *Hind*III can be inserted into this plasmid. The pieces of human DNA are mixed with cut plasmids.

c Which restriction enzyme should be used to cut the plasmids, and why?

d What else must be added to the mixture to form recombinant plasmids?

Bacteria such as *Escherichia coli* are then added to the mixture containing recombinant plasmids. Some of these will take up the recombinant plasmids, some will take up non-recombinant plasmids, and others will not take up a plasmid at all.

e Describe an experimental procedure you could carry out, which would enable you to separate out these three groups of *E. coli*.

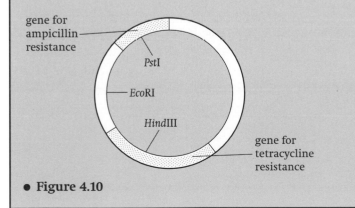

gene for ampicillin resistance

*Pst*I

*Eco*RI

*Hind*III

gene for tetracycline resistance

● **Figure 4.10**

5 The following article appears in your local paper. A friend of yours, who does not study A Level biology, asks you to explain the issues involved, and wants to know whether there is any cause for concern. What will you say to your friend?

A 'superbug' created locally to help boost world food production has prompted fears for public safety

A new microorganism developed at GENBUG Ltd's research unit has been released into local fields, it was revealed this week. The company claims the genetically engineered 'superbug' – capable of transforming poor soil into fertile land yielding bumper crops – is a harmless bacterium. But families living near the test fields have condemned GENBUG's 'cloak and dagger experiments' which they say 'could wreak havoc'.

John Smith, of Clover Avenue, said: 'We sussed that the fields backing onto our gardens were being used for some sort of experiment so we asked GENBUG what was going on. It turns out that freak bugs have been released into the soil. Everyone round here is blazing mad that GENBUG kept quiet about this. If we'd known before we might have been able to stop the fields being used. But now millions of mutant germs must be burrowing their way onto our land, doing God knows what long-term damage to people's health and the environment. I know scientific experiments are necessary but people living so close to these fields should have been consulted about something like this which could affect them directly.'

Mr Smith said GENBUG must have been swamped with protests. 'I've certainly made it very clear to them what I think of their cloak and dagger experiments. We still know nothing about the possible consequences.

I'm worried sick about the harm these bugs could do to my children and I know other parents round here are frightened to let youngsters play in their own gardens now. That can't be right, can it?'

A GENBUG spokesman insisted the field tests were not dangerous. He said: 'The bug we have used is an ordinary bacterium which grows naturally in the soil. But we have changed the organism's genetic blueprint (DNA) to make it very efficient at producing nitrates which plants need to grow.'

He said GENBUG chief scientists were prepared to meet residents to discuss their fears but he added: 'Our so-called superbug is quite harmless and represents no threat to the health of people living in the area. Indeed, GENBUG is proud of its amazing breakthrough in genetic engineering which could well revolutionise farming and play an important role in famine relief.'

6 Anandra Chakrabarty developed a strain of *Pseudomonas* bacterium which carried four different plasmids and could therefore degrade four different components in oil. This made it very efficient at cleaning up oil spills, so he applied for a patent on this bacterium. After much argument, the patent was eventually granted.

A doctor was treating a man from Los Angeles who had hairy cell leukaemia. The doctor removed the patient's spleen and cultured some of the cells artificially. He found that the cells produced several interesting proteins, so he patented the cells and made a considerable amount of money from commercial firms. When the patient discovered that the doctor had obtained a patent on some of his cells, he sued the doctor, but his claim was rejected.

The patient is appealing against the decision.

a Is it right to patent living organisms and tissues?

b Who owns human cells and tissues? Is it the person from whose body they come, or the doctor with the skills to recognise their value?

c Drug companies can charge high prices for their drugs because they own patents, and many people are prepared to buy the drugs because they are desperate to overcome life-threatening disease. Is this morally justified? On the other hand, if companies are not granted patents, how can they recover their considerable research and development costs?

CHAPTER 5

Biotechnology in medicine

By the end of this chapter you should be able to:

1 outline one method for the production of a monoclonal antibody;

2 describe the use of monoclonal antibodies in pregnancy testing;

3 explain the reasons for using microorganisms in processes designed for the large-scale production of human growth hormone and insulin;

4 describe the detailed sequence of steps that can be used to produce a protein of medical importance, such as human growth hormone;

5 discuss the benefits and hazards of genetic engineering with reference to suitable examples;

6 explain what is meant by the term *biosensor*, with reference to the monitoring of blood glucose.

Monoclonal antibody production

Monoclonal antibodies are antibodies against one specific antigen. (You might like to look back to *Biology 1*, chapter 16, to remind yourself about antigens, antibodies and the immune system.) The technique for producing them was discovered in 1975 by Cesar Milstein and Georges Kohler. In order to obtain a cell line that made the desired antibody, they injected mice with the antigen. The mouse then mounted an immune response, and produced B lymphocytes which made antibodies against the specific antigen. After 2–3 weeks, the mouse was killed and the spleen removed. Lymphocytes were washed out and centrifuged to separate them from other blood cells. Among these lymphocytes there would be some producing the desired antibody. However, there was a major problem: lymphocytes do not divide in culture, so it would be difficult to produce antibodies from them. Milstein and Kohler solved this problem by fusing the lymphocytes with **myeloma** cells. These are cancer cells which divide readily in culture. The B lymphocytes from the mouse spleen were fused with myeloma cells this was done using a **fusogen**, which is a chemical, such as polyethylene glycol

(PEG), that causes the membranes of cells to join. Even with a fusogen, only very few lymphocytes hybridised with myeloma cells, and unfused lymphocytes died. The resulting **hybridoma** cells were then cloned. Since all hybrids of the same clone produce the same antibody, they were called monoclonal antibodies. Unfused myeloma cells would be able to survive along with the hybridised cells so, to prevent this, a special medium is used that will only support the growth of the hybridoma cells. The hybridoma cells can secrete antibodies, like the original B lymphocytes, but in addition they can be cloned, in suspension, and will divide rapidly. However, of all the hybridoma cells, very few will secrete the particular antibody needed.

It is necessary to clone the cells and test them to see whether any of the surviving hybridomas secretes the desired antibody. The medium is diluted and divided so that an average of one cell only is added to each of the wells on a multi-well culture dish (*figure 5.1*). After about a week, each well will contain about 10 000 identical hybridoma cells. A tiny sample is tested from each one to see whether the desired antibody has been produced. If it is found, cells from that well will

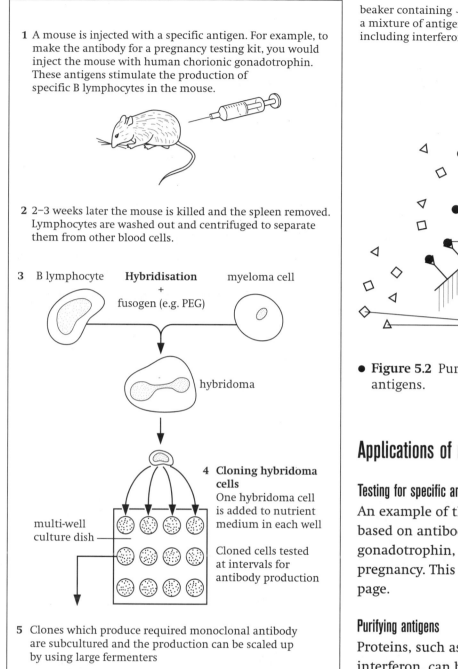

1 A mouse is injected with a specific antigen. For example, to make the antibody for a pregnancy testing kit, you would inject the mouse with human chorionic gonadotrophin. These antigens stimulate the production of specific B lymphocytes in the mouse.

2 2–3 weeks later the mouse is killed and the spleen removed. Lymphocytes are washed out and centrifuged to separate them from other blood cells.

3 B lymphocyte   **Hybridisation**   myeloma cell
                        +
              fusogen (e.g. PEG)

                    hybridoma

4 **Cloning hybridoma cells**
One hybridoma cell is added to nutrient medium in each well

multi-well culture dish

Cloned cells tested at intervals for antibody production

5 Clones which produce required monoclonal antibody are subcultured and the production can be scaled up by using large fermenters

● **Figure 5.1** Monoclonal antibody production.

be cloned, on as large a scale as possible, to produce monoclonal antibodies.

SAQ 5.1
Explain why   **a** unfused lymphocytes die;
b lymphocytes need to be fused with myeloma cells.

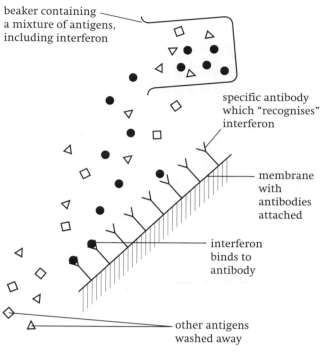

beaker containing a mixture of antigens, including interferon

specific antibody which "recognises" interferon

membrane with antibodies attached

interferon binds to antibody

other antigens washed away

● **Figure 5.2** Purifying interferon from a mixture of antigens.

Applications of monoclonal antibodies

Testing for specific antigens
An example of this is in pregnancy testing kits, based on antibodies to human chorionic gonadotrophin, a hormone produced only during pregnancy. This is covered in detail on the next page.

Purifying antigens
Proteins, such as enzymes or the anti-viral drug interferon, can be separated from a mixture of substances by passing the mixture over a surface containing specific monoclonal antibodies. In this process, the protein is acting as an antigen, and can be purified by removal from the antibodies (*figure 5.2*).

'Magic bullets' anti-cancer drugs
Monoclonal antibodies have been developed which bind specifically with cancer cells. Drugs are bonded to the monoclonal antibodies so that these drugs specifically target cancer cells. This minimises any side-effects and prevents damage to healthy cells.

Diagnosis of infectious diseases

Monoclonal antibodies can detect antigens, such as viruses or bacterial toxins, in samples of body fluids. They are now in use for the rapid diagnosis of the sexually transmitted disease (STD) gonorrhoea. It was difficult to distinguish between the STD caused by the bacterium *Neisseria gonorrhoea* and that caused by a protozoan parasite called *Chlamydia*, which does not respond to antibiotics. Doctors had to culture the bacteria from a swab, which takes about two days. *Chlamydia* can only be cultured in living cells so the test for it took several days to complete. Two separate tests therefore had to be done and there was a considerable delay in getting the results. Now, tests using monoclonal antibodies have been developed that distinguish between the bacterial and protozoan antigens. They can give a positive diagnosis in only 20 minutes. This allows the correct treatment to be given almost immediately.

Manufacture of passive vaccines

Monoclonal antibodies to combat a pathogen can be injected directly into the patient's blood, or they may be used to suppress a patient's own immune system, for example following an organ transplant.

Pregnancy testing

Monoclonal antibodies are often used to detect the presence of certain chemicals. Readily available from most chemists is the 'dipstick' type of pregnancy testing kit. Pregnant women secrete the

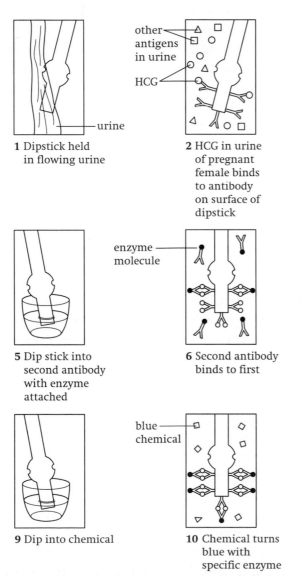

1 Dipstick held in flowing urine

2 HCG in urine of pregnant female binds to antibody on surface of dipstick

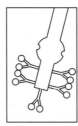

3 Rinse under tap

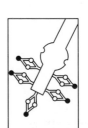

4 HCG has bound to antibody on dipstick. All other antigens washed away

5 Dip stick into second antibody with enzyme attached

6 Second antibody binds to first

7 Rinse again in tap water

8 Antibody with enzyme now attached

9 Dip into chemical

10 Chemical turns blue with specific enzyme

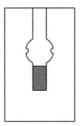

11 Dipstick appears blue – a positive pregnancy test

12 All antibody complex now appears blue

● **Figure 5.3** Monoclonal antibodies in use in a pregnancy testing kit.

hormone human chorionic gonadotrophin (HCG) in their urine. This hormone is produced by the placenta, so it can only be present if a woman is pregnant. In the version of the test shown in *figure 5.3*, the monoclonal antibody to HCG is incorporated into the surface coating of a plastic dipstick. This dipstick is placed in a sample of the pregnant woman's urine. If HCG is present, it binds to the antibody. Excess HCG or any other antigens are removed by washing the dipstick. Next, the dipstick is dipped into a solution containing a second antibody with an enzyme bound to it. This will only bind to the dipstick if there is HCG attached to it. Now the dipstick is dipped into a chemical that will turn blue in the presence of the enzyme, indicating that the woman is pregnant.

SAQ 5.2

Explain why the dipstick will not turn blue if the woman is not pregnant.

Making human proteins

Many **human proteins** can now be produced in culture, by introducing the necessary gene into the DNA of a yeast or bacterium. Among human proteins being made in this way are interleukins and interferon, both of which have an effect on the immune system. Interleukins are synthesised by activated macrophages and stimulate the immune response (see *Biology 1*, chapter 16). Interferon is made by virus-infected cells and protects other cells from becoming infected by viruses. Both interleukins and interferon have potential benefits in cancer therapy.

Human growth hormone is a protein that is produced by the pituitary gland and regulates normal growth. Some children suffer from dwarfism because they lack this hormone and are unable to grow properly unless treated with it. Until recombinant human growth hormone was available the hormone was extracted from pituitary glands obtained from human corpses. However, the hormone produced this way was linked to the transmission of Creutzfeld–Jacob

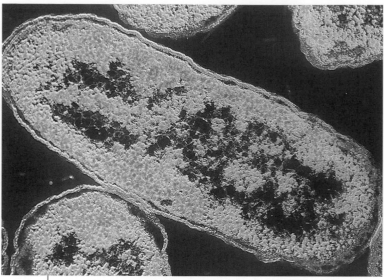

● **Figure 5.4** Transmission electron micrograph of *E. coli* (×60 000).

disease (CJD), which is caused by an infectious protein (a prion) that slowly causes irreversible degeneration of the brain. This source of growth hormone has therefore been withdrawn. Using genetic engineering techniques the gene for human growth hormone has been inserted into bacterial cells so that growth hormone can be produced on a large scale (*figures 5.4* and *5.5*). The hormone is used to treat children suffering from dwarfism. In the US it can also be used for those who are short in stature for other reasons and as an anti-ageing treatment. It is also being considered for use in treating the loss of protein and wasting that follows severe disease and injury.

While this technique was being developed, it was discovered that most people who needed treatment with growth hormone did not actually lack growth hormone itself, but another protein called **growth hormone releasing factor** (GRF). In normal people, GRF is produced in tiny amounts by the hypothalamus, and causes growth hormone to be released from the pituitary gland. Recombinant GRF can also be produced by genetic engineering and is now regarded as the best way to treat most growth deficiencies.

There is some controversy about using human growth hormone made in this way. It may be useful to increase the stature of small children with a deficiency of growth hormone, who might otherwise suffer from dwarfism. However, there are concerns that some parents might pressurise

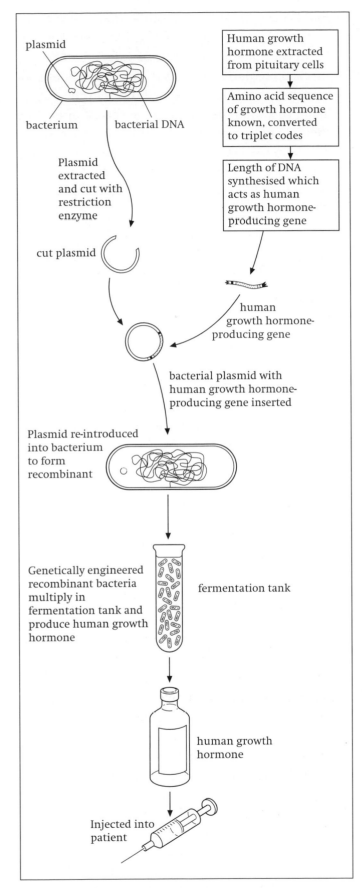

plasmid

bacterium   bacterial DNA

Plasmid extracted and cut with restriction enzyme

cut plasmid

Human growth hormone extracted from pituitary cells

Amino acid sequence of growth hormone known, converted to triplet codes

Length of DNA synthesised which acts as human growth hormone-producing gene

human growth hormone-producing gene

bacterial plasmid with human growth hormone-producing gene inserted

Plasmid re-introduced into bacterium to form recombinant

Genetically engineered recombinant bacteria multiply in fermentation tank and produce human growth hormone

fermentation tank

human growth hormone

Injected into patient

● **Figure 5.5** Flow chart for the manufacture of human growth hormone using genetic engineering techniques.

doctors to prescribe growth hormone to children who are shorter than average, but nevertheless of normal height, for cosmetic reasons.

The human protein **insulin**, which is given to diabetics to control blood glucose level is also now made by genetic engineering. The only source of insulin used to be from cattle and pig pancreases. This meant that supply of the hormone depended on a regular supply of pancreases from slaughtered animals. It also meant that some patients became allergic to the hormone because their bodies recognised it as a non-human protein and mounted an immune response. Genetically engineered human insulin is now being produced on a large scale, by inserting the human gene sequence into a bacterium (as we saw in *Biology 1*, chapter 5). This has the advantage that the engineered product closely resembles human insulin and produces fewer side-effects than the insulin prepared from animal pancreatic extracts.

Other diseases which result from deficiencies of particular proteins may also benefit from developments in recombinant DNA techniques. **Haemophilia** is a hereditary disease in which the blood fails to clot properly. Most haemophiliacs lack a protein called **factor VIII**, and to prevent bleeding had to be treated with factor VIII obtained from human blood. Unfortunately, many haemophiliacs developed AIDS in the early 1990s because they received factor VIII obtained from blood infected with HIV. Although blood donated by donors can now be screened for HIV, many haemophiliacs feel much safer receiving the genetically engineered product.

Erythropoietin is another genetically engineered product which is helping many people. This hormone is produced by healthy kidneys and stimulates red blood cell production (erythropoiesis) in the bone marrow. Many patients with kidney failure do not produce enough erythropoietin from their damaged kidneys, which leads to anaemia (lack of red blood cells). Some of these patients have red blood cell levels which are 50% lower than in normal people, which means they suffer debilitating weakness and tiredness. Previously the only treatment was regular blood transfusions. The gene for erythropoietin has now been cloned, and inserted into Chinese hamster ovary cells. These cells are easy to grow in culture and several copies of the gene have been inserted, making them highly productive. The cells are grown in large fermenters, and the erythropoietin extracted from the culture medium has greatly improved the quality of life for kidney patients.

SAQ 5.3 _____

Sketch a flow chart showing the production of factor VIII by genetic engineering. (You may like to look back to *Biology 1*, chapter 5)

The use of animals as organ donors

There is a serious shortage of human organs available for transplant operations, and thousands of people die every year because of this. One possible solution would be to use animal organs for transplant operations. However, when a person receives an organ transplant, the body's immune system recognises the new organ as 'foreign'. The immune system can attack and destroy the implant, causing rejection. This is more likely to be a problem if animal organs are used, since they are more 'foreign' than an organ from a human donor would be. Early attempts to use animal organs for transplant ended in disaster.

However, over the last decade transplantation of animal organs into humans has become a realistic goal. Pigs have been widely used in this research, because pig organs are similar in size to human organs, and work in a similar way. Furthermore, it is possible to breed pigs that are free of every known disease. Scientists are trying to use genetic engineering techniques to make the donor animal organ match a human organ as closely as possible. If this can be achieved, it could result in a match even closer than using a human donor organ, reducing or even eliminating the need for immune-suppressing drugs after the operation.

There are some concerns about using pigs as organ donors in this way. Some people feel it is unethical to breed animals for this purpose. There are also fears that these pigs may harbour viruses which we do not yet know about. Such viruses

could cause serious diseases in humans. It has been recommended that people receiving pig organ transplants, and their families, should be checked regularly for signs of virus infection, and that they should not have children. On the other hand, this could be a solution to the chronic shortage of human donor organs. There are also people in need of a transplant who feel it is wrong to accept an organ from another human and would have less of an ethical dilemma accepting a pig heart.

Using plants to produce vaccines

Traditionally, vaccines have been produced by growing the disease-causing organism (or pathogen) in culture. The pathogen is either cultured as an attenuated or 'weakened' strain, or it is treated with heat or chemicals to produce a 'killed' vaccine (see *Biology 1*, chapter 16). However, some pathogens are very difficult to grow in culture. It is also hazardous to grow large numbers of disease-causing organisms, and strict safety procedures must be followed. One way to avoid these problems is to use genetic engineering. Research is currently taking place into using plants to produce vaccines.

First, the parts of the pathogen (the antigens) that stimulate antibody formation need to be identified. Sections of DNA which code for these antigens can then be inserted into plants, such as bananas. The bananas then synthesise the antigen and can be eaten by children as an oral vaccine, saving them the pain and distress of an injection. This method is likely to produce cheaper vaccines, making it possible to provide them to children all round the world. A further advantage is that, unlike many conventional vaccines, plant-based vaccines do not need refrigeration. The advantages of this kind of vaccine are not limited to humans: researchers in the US and Canada are testing vaccines that can be put in corn and soybeans to feed to animals.

SAQ 5.4 _____

Suggest how a gene coding for an antigen is inserted into a banana.

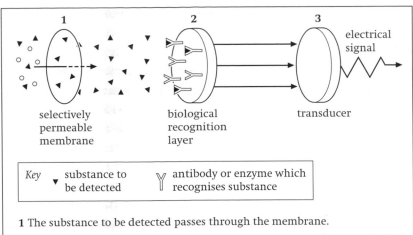

Key ▼ substance to be detected   Y antibody or enzyme which recognises substance

1 The substance to be detected passes through the membrane.

2 The substance binds to the recognition layer which may contain antibodies or enzymes; a reaction takes place.

3 The product of the reaction passes to a transducer and thus produces an electrical signal.

● **Figure 5.6** The parts of a biosensor.

Biosensors

In order to survive, living things must be able to respond to changes in the environment, to detect food or to avoid toxic chemicals. Biological sensory systems can be extremely sensitive. 'Sniffer' dogs are able to detect the trail of humans, illegal drugs or explosives, while sharks can detect small amounts of blood from hundreds of metres away. In chapter 4, we saw how it might be possible to create new living **biosensors** to monitor crop conditions (page 55).

A biosensor is a device that uses a biological molecule, to detect and measure a chemical compound. In a biosensor there is a **biological recognition layer**, which may be an enzyme or enzymes, an antibody, a membrane component, an organelle, a prokaryotic or eukaryotic cell, or even living tissues. This layer is used to recognise a particular substance by producing a biochemical signal. The biological component is the part which ensures sensitivity and is responsible for the high degree of specificity shown by biosensors. The basis of the sensor is that, when two biological molecules interact, there are measurable physical or chemical changes, which can be measured by a transducer. The biological component is immobilised on to the surface of the transducer so that these changes can be measured accurately (*figure 5.6*).

The **transducer** is an electrical device which can measure the signals from the biological reaction. Most transducers fall into two categories, potentiometric electrodes, which do not have any voltage applied, and amperometric electrodes, which have a constant applied voltage. Both types measure the voltage produced by the physical or chemical reaction. A familiar type of potentiometric electrode is the standard pH electrode. An enzyme can be immobilised on a membrane, which is placed over the pH electrode and specifically measures substrates or products as they are broken down or produced on the electrode surface. An example of an amperometric electrode is the oxygen concentration electrode. (You can read more about **immobilisation** in chapter 6.) However, some biosensors are being developed in which the immobilised enzyme is close to a thermistor (temperature sensor), and the heat evolved during the biological reaction is measured. Clearly these can only be used when the external temperature is constant.

The first attempt to make a biosensor was in the 1960s when a sensor was developed which allowed surgeons to monitor blood glucose levels continuously during surgery. In this sensor the enzyme glucose oxidase was used. This catalyses the reaction between glucose and oxygen in solution to form gluconic acid and hydrogen peroxide. The enzyme was associated with a platinum oxygen electrode which measured the changing oxygen concentration as blood glucose levels changed.

Optical fibre biosensors

A different approach involves the use of optical fibre technology. Antibodies can be tagged with fluorescent molecules and deposited on the surface of an optical fibre. When light travels along an optical fibre it is reflected back off the outer layer as shown in *figure 5.7*. At the points of internal reflection, some of the light energy is transmitted outwards and when it meets the antibody layer some of it is deflected back into the fibre as fluorescence.

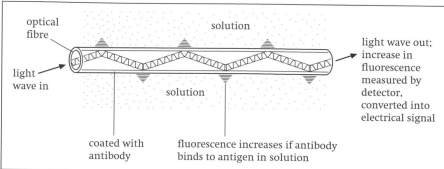

optical fibre

solution

light wave in

light wave out; increase in fluorescence measured by detector, converted into electrical signal

coated with antibody

solution

fluorescence increases if antibody binds to antigen in solution

● **Figure 5.7** Optical fibre biosensor.

The fluorescence increases when the antibody binds with its antigen. The intensity of the resulting light can be detected by a sensor and converted into an electrical signal. This enables the presence of antigens to be detected in a sample of body fluid. Alternatively, the optical fibre can be coated with antigen and used to detect the presence of antibody. In the future, it should be possible to obtain an immediate indication of the presence of antibodies such as those produced in response to the HIV virus.

Microchip biosensors

Recently biosensors have been developed where the transducer is a microchip. One example is a biosensor, smaller than a ballpoint pen, that has been developed to detect the level of glucose in blood – a modern version of the very first biosensor. The enzyme glucose oxidase is incorporated into a disposable probe that clips into the electrical device, and the tip of the probe is dipped into a drop of blood. Glucose oxidase reacts with glucose in the sample to produce gluconic acid, which generates an electric current in the chip. The current is relative to the amount of glucose present. It can also give warning of low blood glucose levels (hypoglycaemia). This makes it easier for a diabetic to calculate the dose of insulin needed. Similar sensors for alcohol and cholesterol are being developed.

Further development has produced probes where the enzyme is immobilised on the surface of a silicon chip, making a **biochip**. Such biosensors are very tiny, some 2 mm across, and again one has been developed to detect blood glucose levels. When a positive charge forms on the surface of the chip, due to the gluconic acid

produced, electrons flow to produce a signal which can be processed. As biochips are small and self-contained they are not easily damaged and can both respond to and process the signal. They can be used continuously, so it may soon be possible to implant a small glucose biosensor under the skin. This could control the release of insulin into the bloodstream automatically and act as an 'artificial pancreas'.

SAQ 5.5
Explain how a biosensor might be used to control insulin release in a person with diabetes.

SAQ 5.6
Design, in outline only, a biosensor which might be used to monitor cholesterol or alcohol levels in human blood.

Other uses of biosensors

Food, such as meat, may look fit to eat but may have been kept for too long in unsuitable conditions and may contain too many potentially harmful microorganisms such as *Salmonella*. Until recently, there was no immediate test of food freshness as the culture and identification of contaminating microorganisms generally takes several days. Now, however, a biosensor probe has been developed to detect the numbers of micro-organisms in meat for use in the food industry. It consists of a sharp metal probe containing a biosensor which can be inserted into the meat. The biosensor measures the overall concentration of a range of different sugars in the meat. There is a correlation between sugar concentration and the number of microorganisms which feed on the meat. If the reading is above a certain level, then the meat is declared unsafe for human consumption.

This technique has many future applications and may be used to test the freshness of a wide range of food products. It has the advantage of giving an immediate result, vital in today's 'fast food' industry. It may soon be available for use in food preparation areas and supermarkets and should lead to a higher level of food safety.

Another use for biosensors could be to monitor processes in fermentation such as the build-up of waste products, changes in pH and availability of nutrients. These could be done with great accuracy and would assist with feedback control.

Biochips can also be used to monitor changes in the environment. For example microorganisms that react with heavy metals and organic toxins could be used in the biochips. It may soon be possible to produce a range of biosensors, each incorporating a different microorganism, in order to monitor drinking water, or detect toxic gases, drugs or explosives. These would be very useful in pollution control and forensic science.

A Japanese company is manufacturing toilets which incorporate biosensors to measure glucose levels. When the patient urinates, a small amount of urine is trapped in a section of the toilet bowl and is directed into a chamber containing a glucose biosensor. The biosensor contains glucose oxidase which oxidises any glucose in the urine. The fall in dissolved oxygen is detected by an electrode. It is not yet possible to make a re-usable biosensor which is also reliable, so cheap, disposable biosensors are used. Nevertheless, each test will be much cheaper than hospital tests. Initially the toilets will be used in such places as geriatric day-care centres to detect diabetes, but they have the potential for general health screening. In the future it may be possible to incorporate a multiple biosensor to monitor simultaneously glucose, lactate (an indicator of stress), urea and uric acid (indicators of kidney disease), haemoglobin (which indicates bleeding), antibodies (indicating infections or cancer) and protein concentration (which indicates the functioning of the digestive system). It might also be possible to monitor substances in faeces and sweat. For instance, a skin biosensor, resembling a wristwatch, could be used to monitor fatigue and blood alcohol levels in lorry, bus and taxi drivers.

SUMMARY

◆ Monoclonal antibodies are antibodies specific to one antigen. These may be mass-produced in fermenters.

◆ Monoclonal antibodies have a number of important uses. One important use is in medicine, where they can be used to make diagnostic testing kits, e.g. pregnancy testing kits.

◆ Many human proteins can be produced in culture by inserting the necessary gene into the DNA of a bacterial or yeast cell. Recombinant human growth hormone is used to treat children suffering from dwarfism. Other useful proteins made in this way are human insulin, factor VIII for treating haemophilia, and erythropoietin which stimulates red blood cell production.

◆ Genetic engineering techniques are being used to solve many problems in medicine. There are, however, some important health, safety and ethical considerations: for example, concerning the use of genetically engineered pigs as donors of organs for use in humans.

◆ Biosensors are sensors that contain a biological component, such as an antibody or enzyme. These can be used to monitor such things as blood glucose levels and the progress of a fermentation. There are many other potential uses of biosensors, for example in monitoring water quality, and detecting toxins, drugs and explosives.

Questions

1   Imagine that you are a scientist working for a company that makes biosensors. Make a three-dimensional model of a biosensor that could be used to explain the technique to a customer with very little scientific knowledge.

2   In the future, it might be possible for large employers to incorporate multiple biosensors in the company's toilets, to monitor such things as stress levels, general health indicators, alcohol and drug consumption, and so on. Would you welcome this, as a way of improving people's health, or would it be an infringement of personal freedom? Discuss.

3   *Figure 5.8* shows a simple biosensor which can be used to measure the concentration of glucose in a solution.
    a   Explain how this biosensor works.
    b   Describe two advantages of using a similar biosensor to measure glucose levels in a blood sample, rather than using a chemical test such as Benedict's test (which is described in *Biology 1*, chapter 2).

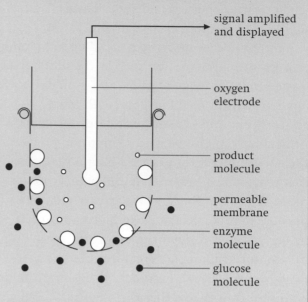

● **Figure 5.8**

4   'Genetic engineering is a technique which can bring great benefits to humans, but also poses considerable risks.' How far would you agree with this statement? You should use material from chapter 4 as well as chapter 5 to answer this question.

5   A company has asked you to design a dipstick-type test kit which could be used to find out whether any of their employees has been using a particular illegal substance. Design a suitable test kit. You may assume that residues of the illegal substance are present in the urine of a person who has been using it.

CHAPTER 6

Biotechnology in industry and public health

By the end of this chapter you should be able to:

1 explain the technique of *enzyme immobilisation*;

2 explain the advantages of enzyme immobilisation in manufacturing industries;

3 carry out an experiment to demonstrate the use of immobilised enzymes, such as amylase immobilised in alginate;

4 describe the use of microorganisms for the treatment of *domestic* and *industrial wastes*;

5 describe the use of named microorganisms and substrates in the production of *biogas* and *gasohol*.

Enzymes are biological catalysts, that is they accelerate the rate of chemical reactions (*Biology 1*, chapter 3). Enzymes are proteins and, in general, very specific, only catalysing one type of reaction and working on only one type of substrate. Substrates are converted to products through the formation of an intermediate enzyme–substrate complex. Many different enzymes are produced by living organisms and, in the field of biotechnology, microorganisms are now proving to be a readily available source of enzymes.

Without knowing it, humans have used enzymes for thousands of years, for making bread, beer, wine and cheese. At the start of this century, they were used commercially by Dr Otto Rohm who was trying to develop an improved method of softening animal skins and removing hairs before tanning to make leather. At the time, pigeon droppings and even dog faeces were used. Rohm found that the active components in these excreta were proteases, enzymes that digest proteins such as trypsin. He found that extracts from animal organs were successful and began to use enzymic extracts from pig and cattle pancreas, a less smelly and dangerous alternative.

SAQ 6.1

Suggest some other enzymes that would be present in the animal excreta used in the tanning industry.

The development of microbial enzyme technology is comparatively recent. Now there is large-scale production of enzymes from microorganisms to catalyse a range of reactions at lower temperatures and pressures than would otherwise be required. Some of the uses of enzyme technology in industry are listed in *table 6.1*.

Since enzymes are proteins, they may be denatured by extremes of temperature and pH. However, industrial enzymes must be very robust and able to withstand a wide range of working conditions. For example they must be able to tolerate a wide temperature range, 10–55 °C, with an optimum around 40 °C. They must also have a wide pH tolerance as they may need to work in the presence of chemicals, such as sulphur dioxide, that usually inhibit enzyme action. Therefore the organisms grown for their enzymes must be selected carefully for these qualities. Indeed, some enzymes have exceptional properties, such as α-amylase which can degrade starch at over 100 °C.

Industry	Enzyme	Use
Dairy industry	animal-derived rennin	cheese manufacture (rennin can only be taken from very young animals, as rennin production decreases with age)
	microbial rennin	increasingly used as a substitute for animal rennin (more acceptable to vegetarians)
	lipases	ripening in blue cheeses by extracellular lipases from mould, e.g. *Penicillium roquefortii*
Brewing industry	amylase and protease enzymes in barley grain	break down starch and proteins in barley grains to sugars and amino acids during malting and mashing stages
	industrially produced amylase, protease, glucanase	break down proteins and polysaccharides in the malt in some breweries
	betaglucanase	breaks down yeast cell walls reducing cloudiness of beer
	protease	breaks down yeast and improves clarity of beer
	amyloglucosidase	breaks down sugars in production of low-calorie beer
Baking industry	proteases	lower protein content of flour for biscuit production
	α-amylase enzymes from yeast	breaks down starch in flour to sugars which can be used by yeast
Biological washing powders	mostly bacterial extracellular proteases	remove organic stains from washing (factory workers may become allergic; encapsulation of enzymes overcomes this)
	amylases	mainly used in dishwasher detergent for removing starch residues
Confectionery industry	α-amylases from *Bacillus subtilis*	produce glucose syrup as a sweetener from waste potato starch; α-amylases break down starch to short glucose chains (dextrins)
	α-amylases from *Aspergillus niger*	hydrolyse dextrins to glucose: enzymes are immobilised and production is continuous; enzymes function for three months and have replaced the older acid hydrolysis method
Agriculture Forestry	ligninases from *Sporotrichum pulverulentum*	most wood waste is not very useful as it contains lignocellulose and few organisms can utilise this: ligninases make cellulose available for animal feed or as an industrial substrate
Textile industry	bacterial amylases	remove starch size, which is used to make fibres smoother, from threads during weaving; these enzymes withstand working temperatures above boiling point
Leather industry	microbial trypsin	removes hair and excess tissue from hides to make leather more pliable (trypsin used to be obtained from dung so microbial trypsin is preferred)
Medical uses	trypsin	dissolves blood clots and cleans wounds
	various enzymes	laboratory diagnosis

● **Table 6.1** Industrial applications of microbial enzyme technology.

Microorganisms have been found to be a valuable source of enzymes, for several reasons:
■ they produce more enzyme molecules in relation to their body mass than most other organisms;
■ they are easy to manipulate genetically and can be subjected to gene transfer techniques;
■ product yield can be increased by means of strain selection, mutation and by optimising growth conditions;

- microorganisms are not influenced by climate and can be grown in suitable laboratories anywhere: this ensures independence of supply from world markets which may be subject to political influence;
- microorganisms can occupy a great variety of habitats and extremes of conditions, so their enzymes show an enormous range of pH and temperature characteristics.

Isolated enzymes

Traditional enzyme technologies, such as beer and cheese manufacture, use the whole micro-organism. However, recent developments use isolated enzymes. This has several advantages:

- when whole organisms are used, some of the substrate is converted to microbial biomass: using isolated enzymes is far less wasteful;
- only one chemical process needs to be considered, so it is much easier to set up the optimum environmental conditions for that process;
- only one enzyme is present, so there will not be wasteful side reactions;
- it is easier to isolate and purify the desired product.

Most industrial enzymes are **extracellular** enzymes, that is those which are secreted by the microorganism into its substrate. These enzymes can easily be extracted from the contents of the fermenter. If **intracellular** enzymes are required, recovery is more complex, since the cells must be disrupted and the desired enzyme extracted from a mixture of many enzymes.

Industrial production of enzymes

Industrial microbiologists have many factors to consider when selecting microorganisms for enzyme production as shown in *figure 6.1*.

When the organism has been selected, genetic engineering may be used to produce a strain which gives a high enzyme yield with other useful properties such as stability. Any less favourable characteristics, such as odour, can be selected against.

Substrates for industrial enzyme technology should be cheap, plentiful and non-toxic.

Commonly used substrates include whey, molasses, and waste starch from flour milling. Table 6.2 lists some of the enzymes and their uses.

SAQ 6.2 _____

What nutrients might be present in the substrates listed above?

SAQ 6.3 _____

Suggest other substrates which might be suitable for industrial enzyme technology.

Enzymes are usually produced by batch culture, although it is sometimes found that better yields are obtained if different substances are added at various times during the fed-batch process.

There are several stages involved in the extraction of extracellular enzymes from the contents of the fermenter (*figure 6.2*):

- filtering off the microorganism;
- concentrating the enzyme by reducing the water content of the liquor;
- removal of bacteria by filtration and addition of antibacterial agents to prevent contamination;
- quality control, to ensure uniformity of the product;
- packaging.

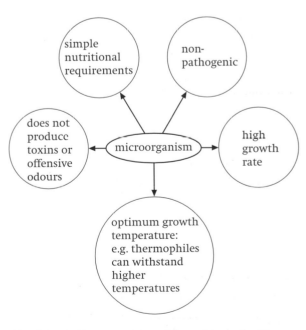

- Figure 6.1 Factors to consider when selecting microorganisms for enzyme production.

Enzyme	Use(s)	Microorganism
α-amylase	breakdown of starch to maltose and dextrins, removing stains from clothes, flour improver, desizing starch on textiles, formation of glucose syrups	*Bacillus subtilis* *Aspergillus oryzae* *Bacillus licheniformis*
β-glucanase	prevents pipe blockage in brewing process by degrading β-glucan in beer, improves clarity of beer	*Aspergillus oryzae* *Bacillus subtilis*
catalase	preservative in drinks	*Aspergillus niger*
cellulase	washing powder, fabric improver and brightener, animal feed production from wastes such as straw	*Penicillium* spp. *Aspergillus* spp.
glucose isomerase	converts glucose to fructose, soft centres in chocolates, soft icing for cakes	*Streptomyces* spp. *Bacillus coagulans*
glucose oxidase	in biosensors to detect glucose in blood of diabetics	*Aspergillus niger*
lactase	conversion of whey to sweeter foods for people who are lactose-intolerant, in sweetened milk drinks, converting lactose to glucose and galactose	*Kluyveromyces lactis*
lipases	in washing powders to digest greasy stains, in cheeses to soften them	*Aspergillus oryzae* (genetically engineered)
pectinase	to extract juice from fruit pulp, to clarify wine and fruit juice	*Erwinia* spp.
protease	used to remove hair and animal tissue from hides in the leather industry, making meat extracts, in biological washing powders to clean protein stains like egg and blood	*Bacillus subtilis*
rennin	baby food manufacture, clotting milk in cheese making	*Kluyveromyces lactis* *Mucor* spp.
sucrase (invertase)	sweet manufacture	*Saccharomyces* spp.
streptokinase	treating bruises and blood clots	*Streptomyces* spp.

● **Table 6.2** Some enzymes produced by microorganisms.

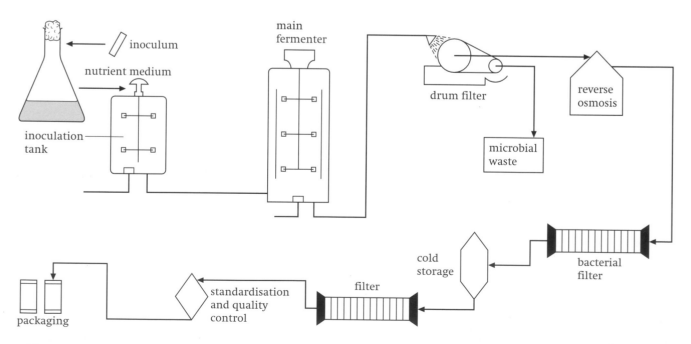

● **Figure 6.2** Extraction of extracellular enzymes.

SAQ 6.4

The water content of the liquor can be reduced by a process called **reverse osmosis**. The liquor flows between membranes, beyond which is a solution with a very low water potential. Use your knowledge of osmosis to explain how this removes water from the liquor. (You may like to look back at *Biology 1*, chapter 4.)

Immobilised enzymes

Recently, methods have been developed where enzymes are attached to insoluble materials that act as a support for the enzyme. The enzymes can then be held in place during the reaction, removed afterwards and used again. This is called **immobilisation** of the enzyme. Sometimes entire microbial cells are immobilised.

Immobilised whole cells are useful because, as it is not necessary to start with a pure enzyme, the process is cheaper and quicker. Whole cells are immobilised in the same way as purified enzymes. They are being used increasingly for complex cultures, such as waste treatment, nitrogen fixation, and the synthesis of steroids, semi-synthetic antibiotics and other medical products.

There are various methods for immobilising enzymes. They can be:

- adsorbed onto an insoluble matrix, such as collagen (*figure 6.3a*);
- held inside a gel, such as silica gel (*figure 6.3b*);
- held within a semi-permeable membrane (*figure 6.3c*);
- trapped in a microcapsule, such as polyacrylamide or alginate beads (*figure 6.3d*).

These processes all involve a physical bonding of the enzyme. They are not easy to carry out and generally result in low enzyme activity. Alternatively, enzymes can be chemically bonded to the support medium (*figure 6.3e*) where enzyme activity is high,

although preparing enzymes in this way is difficult.

The advantages of using immobilised enzymes are:

- enzymes can be recovered and used over and over again, which is particularly useful when the enzyme is expensive or difficult to produce;
- the product will not be contaminated by the enzyme, because the enzyme is held in a matrix;
- the matrix protects the enzyme with a physical barrier, so that it is more stable at extremes of temperature and pH;
- these properties make immobilised enzymes very suitable for continuous culture;
- immobilised enzymes can be controlled more accurately;
- immobilised whole cells mean that several enzymes can participate in the process simultaneously.

Immobilised enzyme technology is still developing rapidly and there are likely to be many new

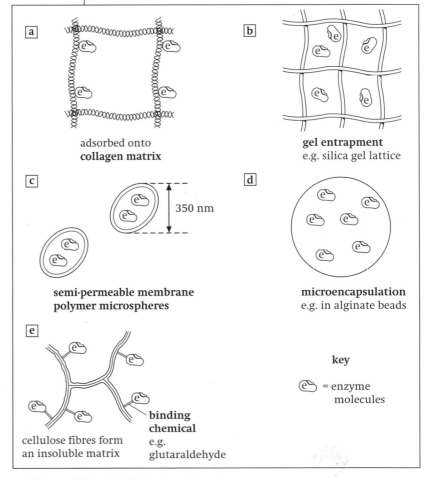

● **Figure 6.3** Immobilisation of enzymes.

applications for immobilised enzymes in industry, medicine and waste disposal.

The production of lactose-free milk

In many parts of the world, milk is an important part of the adult human diet. It contains the disaccharide sugar lactose, which is digested to the monosaccharides glucose and galactose by the enzyme lactase, present in the small intestine. However, there are many adults who lack this enzyme. These people are said to be lactose intolerant. If they drink even a small amount of milk, they suffer severe abdominal cramps, wind, and diarrhoea. Because the lactose does not get digested in the small intestine, it passes through to the colon where bacteria feed on it and produce fatty acids, methane, carbon dioxide and hydrogen. However, immobilised lactase can be used to break down the lactose in milk, making it suitable for lactose intolerant people to drink. Many cats are also lactose intolerant, and it is possible to buy special lactose-free milk for cats in supermarkets. *Figure 6.4* shows how lactose-free milk is made.

Immobilising amylase in alginate beads

Enzymes can be immobilised in the laboratory. One example of this is amylase, which can be immobilised in alginate beads (*figure 6.5*). Amylase enzyme is mixed with sodium alginate. This is then dripped through a syringe barrel into a beaker of calcium chloride solution. The calcium ions displace the sodium ions, forming hard 'beads' of calcium alginate with amylase trapped inside. After the beads have been left to harden, they are rinsed and placed in a column. A starch suspension can be trickled over the beads and collected in a beaker at the bottom of the column. The original starch suspension trickled in at the top gives a positive iodine test but a negative

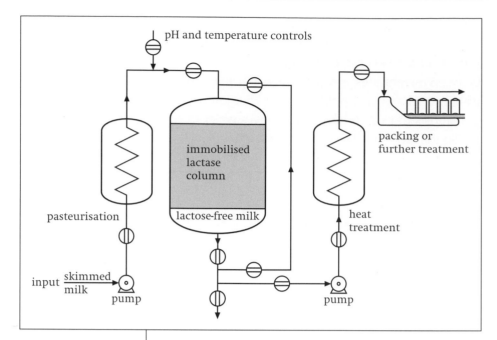

● **Figure 6.4** The production of lactose-free milk.

Benedict's test, showing that there is no maltose present. After passing through the column, the liquid collected gives a negative iodine test but a positive Benedict's test, showing that the starch has been hydrolysed to maltose. (These foods tests are referred to in *Biology 1*, chapter 2.)

SAQ 6.5

a Name a food test you could use to show that the maltose solution produced in this experiment is not contaminated with enzymes.

b Name two variables which would affect the rate of this reaction.

Sewage

Sewage contains:

■ **human waste** made up of human excreta mixed with waste household water. This contains many microorganisms including potential pathogens. A major pollutant from waste household water is detergent, which causes persistent foam and has high levels of phosphates.

■ **industrial wastes**, which are variable, depending on the industry. Some can be very toxic to microorganisms and must undergo pretreatment so that they do not kill or inhibit the microorganisms which degrade the sewage.

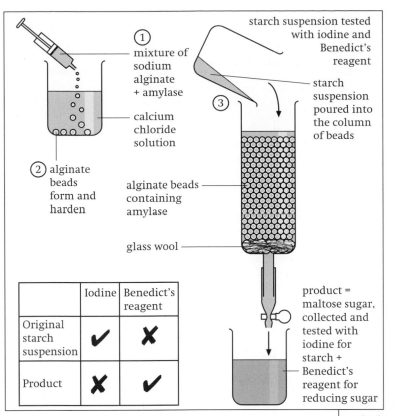

● **Figure 6.5** Making immobilised amylase in the laboratory.

Many industries are required to treat their own sewage, either wholly or partially.

■ **road drainage**, which consists of rain water together with grit and other debris which enters the sewage from roadside gutters.

SAQ 6.6

What toxins might be present in industrial waste?

Sewage treatment

There are two main reasons for treating sewage. Firstly, sewage can contain pathogens which cause diseases, such as *Salmonella typhi* (typhoid), pathogenic *Escherichia coli* (gastroenteritis), and *Ascaris lumbricoides* (roundworm). Secondly, by treating sewage, pollution of the environment can be avoided. Sewage is treated in two or three stages as follows:

■ **primary treatment**. Materials which will settle out are removed. The sedimented solids pass on to a digester for further treatment, while the liquid (effluent) continues into the secondary treatment stage (*figure 6.6*).

■ **secondary treatment**. Aerobic micro-organisms are used to break down most of the organic matter in the effluent. Any sludge produced in this process is passed on to anaerobic digesters.

■ **tertiary treatment**. This involves chemical and biological treatment which renders the sewage effluent fit for drinking. However, this is a very expensive treatment, so it is only carried out when absolutely necessary.

Primary treatment

Sewage is passed through a series of screens to remove large objects, such as boxes and rags, then through a finer screen to remove grit, which could otherwise harm the machinery. The sewage then passes into **sedimentation tanks**. The flow-rate is greatly reduced here, so large organic particles sediment out to form a sludge. The sludge is taken off for anaerobic digestion. The supernatant liquid, or effluent, passes on to the next stage for secondary treatment.

Secondary treatment.

The modern method of secondary treatment, used in large sewage works, is the **activated sludge process**. The organic matter in the sewage is used as a nutrient medium for the growth of a great variety of microorganisms in large tanks (*figure 6.7*). Oxygen levels are kept at a very high level by constantly aerating the sewage, either by bubbling air through it or by rapidly rotating paddles.

The activated sludge tanks contain a complex mixture of microorganisms. Bacteria and fungi tend to break down the sewage into simpler substances. There are many other organisms, such as ciliated protozoa and nematode worms, present in the sludge. These feed off the organic matter in the sludge and digest it to simpler inorganic compounds.

At the end of this process, much of the organic matter has been removed, but a sludge consisting of surplus microorganisms is produced. Some of this sludge is recycled to act as an inoculum for the next batch of effluent, while the rest is anaerobically digested.

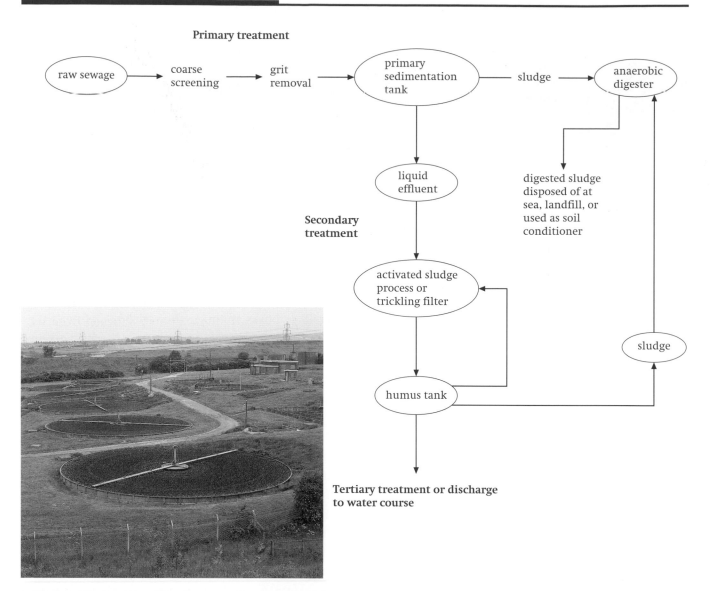

Primary treatment

raw sewage → coarse screening → grit removal → primary sedimentation tank → sludge → anaerobic digester

primary sedimentation tank → liquid effluent

anaerobic digester → digested sludge disposed of at sea, landfill, or used as soil conditioner

Secondary treatment

liquid effluent → activated sludge process or trickling filter → humus tank

humus tank → sludge → anaerobic digester

sludge → activated sludge process or trickling filter

Tertiary treatment or discharge to water course

● **Figure 6.6** A conventional sewage treatment works.

An older method for secondary treatment, still used in smaller sewage works, is the **trickling filter** or **filter bed** (*figures* 6.6 and 6.8). The filter is made of a layer of porous clinker or plastic piping, about 2 m deep. A film of slime-forming bacteria and fungi grows over the surface of the filter bed, together with small invertebrates such as worms, insect larvae and rotifers.

The breakdown of organic matter occurs in a similar way to that described for activated sludge. The slime-forming bacteria and fungi carry out most of

● **Figure 6.7** Sewage treatment: the activated sludge process.

the initial breakdown, with ciliated protozoa feeding off them. This is vital as over-growth of the film can block the filter and reduce oxygen levels. Invertebrates such as the worms and rotifers feed off the protozoa.

After passing through the activated sludge process or the trickling filter, the effluent passes into a humus tank which removes small organic particles that may still remain, together with microbial biomass that has not settled out. This is stuck together into larger particles (floc) by floc-forming bacteria such as *Zoogloea ramigera*, which secrete a sticky polysaccharide. This is then passed to the anaerobic digesters. The effluent from the humus tank is usually discharged into the water course. However, in highly populated areas where the water course is used to supply drinking water, tertiary treatment may be necessary.

SAQ 6.7

Some large sewage works handling considerable quantities of industrial waste, e.g. from the petrochemical industry, have both activated sludge processes and trickling filters. Suggest a reason for this.

Tertiary treatment

The sludge from the sedimentation tanks and from secondary treatment is passed into large tanks where it is digested by anaerobic bacteria. Methane is produced, along with some carbon dioxide. Methane is only produced in strictly anaerobic conditions. The pH must be kept between 6 and 8 and the temperature must not fall below 15 °C. The methane gas produced may be used to heat up the digester tanks. Sometimes the methane is used to generate electricity, which can be used to power the sewage plant.

Digested sludge can be dried. Often it is dumped at sea, or used as landfill to produce methane. Sludge may be spread on farmland as a 'soil conditioner'. It improves the water-retaining quality of the soil and supplies certain mineral salts, such as phosphates and nitrates.

This is only carried out when a very high quality effluent is required, for example, where water will be discharged into a river close to an extraction point for drinking water. Various techniques are used including chemical treatment to remove nitrate and phosphate ions; passing the effluent through rapid gravity sand filters; or the use of reed beds and lagoons. The common reed (*Phragmites* sp.) is able to transfer oxygen from its leaves, down its stem and out through its root system. As a result of this action, a very high population of microorganisms occurs around its roots. The effluent moves slowly past the mass of reed roots and the base of its stem, where the microorganisms complete the breakdown of the sewage effluent.

Other methods of sewage treatment.

- **Septic tanks and pit latrines**. These are small, local ways of dealing with sewage. The microorganisms naturally present in the sewage are used to break down the organic matter. In the case of pit latrines, the environment is able to cope with the comparatively small amount of effluent. In septic tanks, the volume and strength of the sewage is greatly reduced by microbial action. (It is important that householders with septic tanks do not use too much bleach or disinfectants, as these kill the microorganisms and stop treatment taking place in the tank.) The remaining sludge is removed by a tanker at intervals.
- **Sewage lagoons**. This method is used in the Mediterranean and tropics. A series of lagoon lakes is constructed with sewage entering at one end and effluent coming out at the other end.

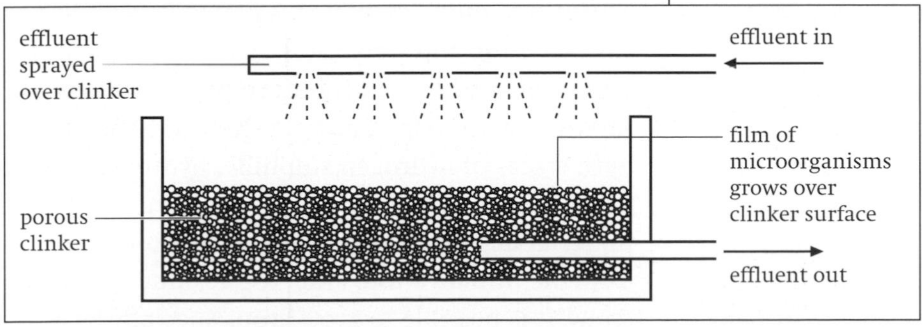

● **Figure 6.8** A simplified diagram of a section through a trickling filter.

Photosynthetic algae aerate the sewage, with anaerobic digestion occurring in the muddy substrate, which contains anaerobic bacteria.

■ **Stabilisation ponds.** This is a variation on the idea of sewage lagoons. A range of large green plants flourish in the organic matter, while microorganisms grow on their roots. These microorganisms feed on the organic matter in the sewage, breaking it down to simpler inorganic substances.

These last two systems give an effluent with lower numbers of microorganisms and fewer pathogens; this is highly desirable in warm countries. They are also seasonal. Summer temperatures increase the rate of sewage breakdown, thereby coping with the increased sewage volume in the summer as a result of tourism.

The production of methane

Methane is a gas which is produced naturally during the anaerobic decay of plant and animal material, such as in the cow's rumen stomach or below the surface of peat bogs. This gas can be used as a replacement for natural gas and research has been carried out to find ways to make it cheaply and economically. The rumen of ruminant animals, such as the cow, is a complex fermentation system with many different microorganisms involved. Attempts to set up similar processes in fermenters need precise monitoring, since it is not easy to imitate the natural process. However, methane production can be done on a very low technology scale, which is suitable for developing countries.

Using sewage

Many sewage treatment plants now have anaerobic digesters for sewage treatment. The sludge is separated from the liquid effluent, which is treated aerobically. The semi-solid sludge is placed in digesters and warmed to 15 °C. Microorganisms naturally present in the sludge, such as *Methanobacterium*, *Methanococcus* and *Methanothrix*, digest the organic sludge and produce methane which can be used to power the sewage treatment plant.

Using urban waste, landfill gas

In recent years in the UK a biofuels programme, with the backing of the Department of Energy, has concentrated on the production and use of gases formed when domestic refuse biodegrades in landfill sites. Refuse is decomposed under anaerobic conditions, using microorganisms such as *Methanobacterium* that are naturally present, to yield a mixture of gases containing large quantities of methane. This is called landfill gas. One successful scheme is at Bidston Moss, Merseyside, UK.

Formerly a peat mossland, Bidston Moss has been used as a waste disposal site for over 50 years, receiving mostly domestic refuse since the mid-1980s. The waste has been tipped to form a mound about 20 m thick and vertical wells have been drilled to collect gas from an area covering about 40% of the site. The gas is transported, via pipelines, to a header pipe which circles the site. The gas flow and yield are controlled by a series of valves. The gas is dried before being piped 2.5 km along a polyethylene pipe, laid one metre underground, to a large factory complex where the gas is used to raise steam in a huge boiler. This site yields 100–150 million megajoules of gas annually. At Bidston Moss, the scheme has proved to be economically viable due to the large volume of gas released and the convenient location nearby of a commercial customer. It has also helped to cut down on the unpleasant smells formerly released from the site. Other local authorities are liquefying landfill gas and using it to run their vehicles.

Biogas fermenters

These have been used for hundreds of years in some countries. In India, Pakistan and China, for example, systems range from very small family schemes to quite large biogas plants (*figure 6.9*). Animal dung and water are allowed to ferment in almost anaerobic conditions, to produce **biogas**, a mixture of methane and carbon dioxide together with traces of hydrogen sulphide, hydrogen and water, which is useful as a fuel. Any organic material may be used in these fermenters, for example human waste and crop residues such as straw. It is possible to grow crops specially as a substrate for methane production. In addition,

● **Figure 6.9** Biogas fermenter in Nepal.

the wastes from methane digesters can be useful by-products. The residue is rich in such nutrients as ammonia and phosphates, and can be used as a soil conditioner or even animal feed. As well as methane, other fuels such as propanol and butanol can be made this way. Utilising digester wastes for soil conditioning increases the cost-effectiveness. However, while this is a useful small-scale process, it is unlikely to be commercially viable on a large scale because:

■ methane can be produced far more cheaply from coal;
■ natural gas is cheaper than microbially produced methane;
■ there are many natural sources of methane;
■ gas is expensive to store, transport and distribute;
■ it is expensive and difficult to liquefy.

Some farms in developed countries now place animal manure and other crop residues into anaerobic digestion tanks. Here, the waste is fermented by microorganisms and the methane produced is collected, liquefied and used to power farm machinery. In some cases it may be used to fire boilers, which heat glasshouses and produce early crops of tomatoes, peppers and other vegetables.

SAQ 6.8

Design a simple biogas fermenter which could safely be used by a family in a developing country.

SAQ 6.9

A semi–solid residue remains after biogas has been produced in a fermenter. Suggest a use for this residue.

Energy from biomass

The world has become increasingly dependent on non-renewable energy sources such as petrol. World oil supplies are predicted to run out in about 50 years and scientists are working to overcome the crisis by finding alternative, preferably renewable, energy sources. Microorganisms offer one solution to this problem.

Biomass is an attractive energy source, since it is formed by photosynthesis using energy from sunlight which is effectively unlimited. At present a great deal of biomass is wasted. Biomass includes straw, timber and crop residues. Microorganisms can make use of these wastes and at the same time help to solve waste disposal problems. In addition, low-tech designs for fuel production are available, for use in developing countries or on a small scale, where traditional energy production methods are less effective.

Almost any organic waste materials can be used to produce fuel. This can be highly cost-effective because such materials are cheap to obtain and using them saves the often high cost of disposal. It is also possible to grow crops specially for energy production on land unsuitable for growing foodstuffs or where the climate is suitable for rapid growth. Sugar cane is already being grown in Brazil for this purpose. In the UK, forestry is likely to be the most useful energy crop, and willow, grasses and new species of rapidly growing conifers are being developed for this purpose.

Gasohol production

Ethanol has been produced by fermentation for thousands of years and as long ago as 1890 it was used as a motor car fuel. In the 1920s and 1930s cars were run on ethanol in some parts of the world and also during the Second World War when there were fuel shortages. At present, most industrial alcohol is made synthetically, from by-products of the petrochemical industry. However, many developing countries have always used traditional fermentation methods to make industrial alcohol, since cheap raw materials are available. As the price of oil increases, this method will become more attractive to industrialised countries. Since alcohol can be converted easily into ethene and other similar compounds, which are the basic raw materials in plastics manufacture, it could replace oil in this industry.

Brazil has made the greatest advances in the production of ethanol by traditional methods, and is currently the world leader in producing fuel alcohol, which is mixed with petrol to give a fuel called **gasohol**. Gasohol is also produced in the USA. Many carbohydrate substrates are used, including sugar cane, cassava roots and cellulose waste. Cassava roots contain starch which must be hydrolysed first to sugars. Cellulose waste, such as

timber and straw, needs quite complex pre-treatment with lignocellulase enzymes or chemicals. The sugar-rich substrate is placed in a fermenter and yeast is added. The yeast ferments the sugars to ethanol, which is obtained from the contents of the fermenter by distillation (*figure 6.10*).

Brazil is building over 500 fermentation and distillation plants and eventually aims to supply the country's entire petrol needs with ethanol. At present, alcohol production is mainly by the traditional process but much research is taking place. It is hoped that more efficient genetically engineered microorganisms will be developed and that newer fermenter designs and immobilised enzyme technology will improve efficiency. Distillation costs can be reduced by using a cheap fuel. For example **bagasse**, the waste from sugar cane, has proved to be economical for raising steam for the process.

Using biomass as a fuel source could help solve another problem. The burning of fossil fuels releases carbon dioxide, which has been locked away for millions of years, into the atmosphere. It

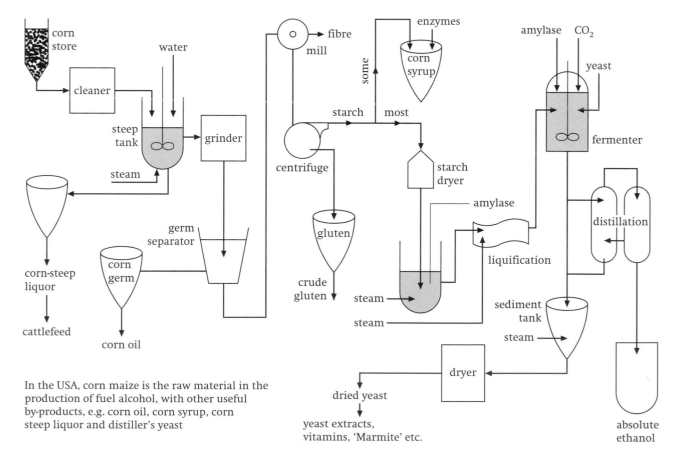

In the USA, corn maize is the raw material in the production of fuel alcohol, with other useful by-products, e.g. corn oil, corn syrup, corn steep liquor and distiller's yeast

● **Figure 6.10** Ethanol production.

is thought that the increased amount of carbon dioxide in the atmosphere might increase the **greenhouse effect**, that is the trapping of infrared rays from the Sun within the atmosphere, and lead to an increase in temperature of the air. This could have many effects, such as changing world weather patterns and melting polar ice caps to raise sea levels. If biomass is used as an alternative, where the carbon dioxide has only recently been fixed in the plant tissue, there would be no net effect on the carbon dioxide levels in the atmosphere.

A range of microorganisms have been used in the production of ethanol, using many different carbohydrates as substrate. Traditionally ethanol production has relied on the use of yeasts, mostly *Saccharomyces* spp. In South America, the fungus *Zygomonas mobilis* has been used for many years in the production of tequila, and in Indonesia and Africa to make palm wine. Recent research has shown that *Zygomonas* is more efficient than yeasts in converting sugar to ethanol. It also produces only trace amounts of glycerol, a major by-product in yeast fermentation, so that there is a higher ethanol yield. The smaller *Zygomonas* cells have a higher surface area to volume ratio and so take up sugar and give out ethanol more quickly than does yeast. Its fermentation rate is faster than yeast and it has a greater ethanol tolerance limit.

A technique has been developed to produce ethanol using *Zygomonas* in continuous culture, rather than by the more traditional batch method. The cells are immobilised on to an inert support medium and packed into a column. The substrate, in solution, flows slowly past. This process seems to be very promising.

At present ethanol is still more expensive than oil, but an increasing number of governments are funding research because of the environmental benefits, and because supplies of oil are limited so that the price of oil will eventually rise substantially.

Microbial mining

Some bacteria are useful in extracting metals from low-grade ores. This is because they are **chemoautotrophic**, which means they derive their energy from inorganic chemicals (see page 25). Bacteria of the genus *Thiobacillus* are used commercially to extract copper and uranium from otherwise uneconomic reserves. Cobalt, lead and nickel may also be extracted in this way in the near future. The extraction process may require extremes of environmental conditions, such as pH and temperature. Genetic engineering is being used to confer acid and heat resistance on these organisms.

Copper mining

In the 1700s Spanish miners knew that they could cause free copper to seep out of piles of copper ore simply by running water over it. What they did not realise was that the moisture allowed bacteria which were naturally present to oxidise the sulphur that was binding the copper in the ore. One of the bacteria responsible for this,

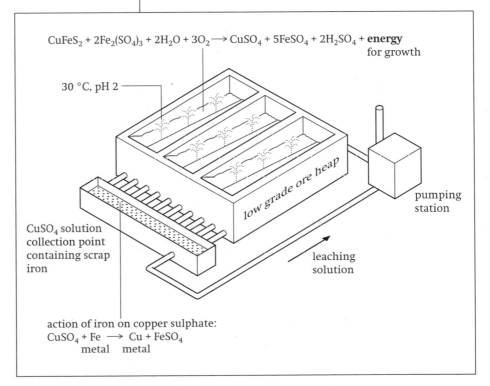

$$CuFeS_2 + 2Fe_2(SO_4)_3 + 2H_2O + 3O_2 \longrightarrow CuSO_4 + 5FeSO_4 + 2H_2SO_4 + \textbf{energy for growth}$$

30 °C, pH 2

low grade ore heap

pumping station

$CuSO_4$ solution collection point containing scrap iron

leaching solution

action of iron on copper sulphate:
$$CuSO_4 + Fe \longrightarrow Cu + FeSO_4$$
$$\text{metal} \qquad \text{metal}$$

● **Figure 6.11** Microbial mining.

Thiobacillus ferrioxidans, can oxidise insoluble chalcopyrites ore ($CuFeS_2$) and convert it to the soluble salt copper sulphate. Sulphuric acid is produced during the process, yet the organism is able to flourish in these highly acidic conditions. Copper can be extracted by reacting the copper sulphate with scrap iron (*figure 6.11*). This method is responsible for about 25% of the copper produced in the US.

Uranium mining

In uranium mining areas it has been found that water collecting in underground pools is a rich source of this radioactive element. This is because microorganisms naturally present on the rock face break down the low-grade uranium ore. This process can be enhanced by pumping the run-off water (i.e. the water that has run over the uranium-containing rocks), containing bacteria such as *Thiobacillus ferrioxidans*, into the mine. The resulting water is pumped out and is rich in uranium ions. This makes extraction economical and reduces environmental damage.

Uranium and copper are not the only metals which can be mined using bacteria. In Brazilian, Australian and South African gold mines, microorganisms are used to treat the raw ore before final processing with cyanide to extract the metal.

Bioaccumulation

Some microorganisms are able to accumulate metals, and this property can be exploited, both for extracting valuable metals from low-grade waste and for detoxifying wastes. Some bacteria, such as *Pseudomonas* spp., can accumulate metallic mercury. *Pseudomonas aeruginosa* accumulates uranium from effluents, while some *Thiobacillus* species accumulate silver.

Oil recovery and oil digestion

Oil recovery

Conventional oil extraction technology can only extract about 50% of the world's subterranean oil reserves. The rest is trapped in rock or is too viscous to pump. Microbial-enhanced oil recovery is a way of recovering more of this trapped oil by the application of microorganisms or their products. Biological compounds may be injected down wells where they can act in several ways. Firstly, surfactants are used to reduce surface tension and release trapped oil by making it more fluid. Emulsan is one such surfactant.

Emulsan is a polysaccharide polymer produced by microorganisms. It is very substrate-specific and acts only on certain hydrocarbons. Such polysaccharide polymers are found in the bacterial capsule, outside the microbial cell wall and membrane. They can be synthesised in batch culture and production is enhanced when there is an excess of carbon substrate in the growth medium.

A second approach is to add a viscosity enhancer, such as xanthan gum, to the water which is pumped down the well so that it is better at pushing oil out of crevices in the rock. *Xanthomonas* is the bacterium which produces xanthan gum and this can be harvested on a large scale using batch culture.

Dealing with oil pollution

There are some species of microorganisms which are able to feed on the hydrocarbons in oil. However, each species is only able to consume a very limited range of hydrocarbons. Several strains of the bacterium *Pseudomonas* occur naturally and can be used in a mixture to clear up oil-contaminated water. Genetic engineering techniques have enabled the production of a 'superbug' which has several 'oil-consuming' genes inserted into one organism. Plasmids containing genes for the biodegradation of naphthalene, xylene, camphor and octane have been combined into one strain of *Pseudomonas* which is still under trial in field conditions.

However, it is unlikely that bacteria could ever cope fully with a major oil pollution disaster, such as the deliberate release of crude oil into the Persian Gulf during the Gulf War. This is because the bacteria only work at the oil–water interface, not throughout the oil slick, which can be quite thick. Also, the rate of bacterial activity depends on the ambient temperature, which can be quite low in parts of the world such as Alaska, which was the site of the Exxon Valdez oil tanker disaster.

There has been some concern about the release of such genetically engineered superbugs into the environment, as would be required if oil slicks were sprayed with a culture of bacteria. In the long term, it is possible to envisage the localised use of such sprays to clear oil from areas such as rock surfaces. The natural process of decay could certainly be enhanced in this way and it would provide a more environmentally friendly method than spraying with detergents which simply emulsify the oil, allowing it to be washed off, but do not degrade it.

SUMMARY

◆ Enzymes are biological catalysts and have been useful for thousands of years in brewing, bread making, cheese making and tanning (leather making).

◆ More recently, it has been found that microorganisms are a particularly good source of enzymes, which have been produced on a large scale.

◆ These specialist enzymes have been used in a variety of industries, and can also be immobilised so that they may be used repeatedly. For example, immobilised amylase can be used to hydrolyse starch to maltose. The resulting maltose is not contaminated with enzyme.

◆ Sewage is made up of human waste, waste household water, industrial wastes and road drainage water and debris. Microorganisms are used in the treatment of sewage to break down (biodegrade) organic substances and reduce potential pathogens.

◆ Microorganisms may also be used to produce biogas rich in methane, from waste products such as sewage, domestic refuse and agricultural residues. Ethanol may be made from crop residues and used as a fuel, for example in car engines. These could be important sources of energy in the future.

◆ Microorganisms may also be used to assist in oil recovery, especially where conventional oil recovery is uneconomic, and in mining, to extract metals from low-grade ore and to detoxify wastes.

Questions

1 Why are microorganisms particularly suitable as a source material for enzyme production?

2 Construct a table, using the headings below, listing as many examples as possible:

Substrate	Microorganism	Enzyme	Use

3 Where could a scientist look for bacteria and fungi which might be a source of a useful enzyme? How would the scientist then attempt to increase enzyme production by the organism concerned?

4 Outline the main steps in the industrial preparation of a named enzyme.

5 The enzyme xylanase is now being used instead of chlorine to bleach paper. Suggest **two** advantages of using xylanase.

6 What advantages are there in using immobilised enzymes? Give **two** examples of their use.

7 Increasingly, immobilised whole microbial cells are being used as biocatalysts. Why is this an important production process?

8 What environmental and ecological benefits are there in tapping landfill sites for methane production?

9 Suppose you own 20 ha of seaside land that you want to develop into holiday chalets. The property is in a conservation area, so you are required to provide safe and effective sewage treatment. Furthermore, the site is one of outstanding natural beauty, so you must take this into consideration. What are the advantages and disadvantages of each of the following:
   a individual septic tanks for each building;
   b trickling filter;
   c sewage lagoon system?
Would your answers be different if the seaside development was on the Mediterranean coast?

10 Plan a system for sewage disposal that could be used in a space station.

Answers to self-assessment questions

Chapter 1

1.1 The capsule and the flagellum.

1.2

Plasmid = circular piece of DNA not joined to chromosome

mesosome = infolding of membrane, probably used in cell division

cell wall = the main component of this is the peptidoglycan murein

capsule = slimy layer surrounding some bacterial cell walls

pilus = made of pilin, used in conjugation in some species

1.3 Blue-greens are prokaryotic because they are approximately $2\,\mu m$ in diameter, lack a true nucleus, have a naked coil of DNA, with a cell wall similar to that of Gram-negative bacteria, 70S ribosomes, and pigments not in chloroplasts but incorporated into infoldings of the plasma membrane, called lamellae.

1.4 Blue-greens have a very primitive structure, are found ubiquitously in water and damp places, and are primary colonisers of bare ground. In the primitive atmosphere of Earth little free oxygen was available, so the earliest life-forms on Earth are thought to have been similar to the blue-green bacteria, that is, prokaryotic, photosynthetic organisms. Fossil remains of organisms resembling the blue-greens have been found dating from around three billion years ago.

1.5 Features shared by the four phyla of protozoa include:
cytoplasm which can exist in the two states, plasmasol and plasmagel; phagocytosis; contractile vacuoles; food vacuoles; reproduction by binary fission; gas exchange by diffusion across cell membrane; nitrogenous waste is ammonia.

Distinguishing features: Rhizopoda are able to move using pseudopodia; Zoomastigina move using flagella; Ciliophora have many cilia which are organelles of locomotion; Apicomplexa are parasitic and some have different forms during their life cycle in the human and the mosquito; Ciliophora have two types of nucleus.

1.6
a Ascomycota: septate hyphae, asexual reproduction by non-motile spores called conidia borne on conidiophores, sexual reproduction by fusion of the male antheridium with the female ascogonium. Yeasts are also ascomycetes, differing from other fungi in being unicellular and having a cell wall composed largely of polymers of glucan and mannan.

b Basidiomycota: septate hyphae, asexual reproduction usually absent, sexual reproduction by fusion of hyphae of two mating types resulting in fruiting body called basidiocarp bearing basidiospores.

c Zygomycota: aseptate hyphae, asexual reproduction by non-motile spores within a sporangium borne on a sporangiophore, sexual reproduction by fusion of gametangia to form a zygospore.

1.7
a In common with higher plants: eukaryotic cell structure and a cell wall.

b Different from higher plants: cell wall is made of chitin, not cellulose; lack chlorophyll and do not photosynthesise; not composed of separate cells (even when hyphae are septate, there are usually several nuclei in each compartment).

1.8 *Hypha:* filament of a fungus, surrounded by chitinous cell wall and containing cytoplasm and organelles.
Mycelium: filaments of fungus forming an interwoven mass.
Septum: cross wall formed in hyphae of some fungi, dividing the cytoplasm into compartments.

Bud: a daughter yeast cell being formed from the parent cell.

Basidium: a cell in the fruiting body of basidiomycete fungi which bears basidiospores.

1.9 The lytic cycle brings about the sudden death or lysis of the host cell, whereas the lysogenic cycle does not destroy the host cell immediately. In the lytic cycle, the viral DNA causes the host cell to reproduce viruses, whereas the lysogenic cycle incorporates the viral nucleic acid into the host cell DNA so that it is passed on to each daughter cell every time the host cell divides.

1.10 Viruses contain nucleic acid like other living things, but have many non-living features. They do not have a cell structure; they can only reproduce themselves within other living cells; outside a cell they are rather like crystals; they have DNA or RNA but never both; they have no metabolism.

Chapter 2

2.1 **a** Complex – it contains meat extract, which is of unknown chemical composition.

b Meat extract and peptone.

c Meat extract and peptone (amino group in proteins).

d There will be some trace mineral ions in tap water which organisms may need for growth.

e To ensure the medium is at the correct pH for the organisms' enzymes. It also ensures that the medium is neutral, since microorganisms produce acids as they respire.

2.2 **a** (i) Potato dextrose agar is a complex medium, whereas Czapek–Dox agar is a synthetic medium.

(ii) Potato dextrose agar: glucose and potato are the main carbon sources. The nitrogen source will be nitrates and amino groups from proteins in the potato tissue. Mineral salts and other growth factors will be present in the potato tissue.

Czapek–Dox agar: sucrose is the carbon source, and sodium nitrate is the nitrogen source. The other ingredients are mineral salts.

b (i) Czapek–Dox agar is necessary here. You would need to modify the medium to make a number of variants, such as use potassium nitrate instead of sodium nitrate to find the effect of sodium ions on the growth of fungi.

(ii) If environmental factors only are being varied (such as light intensity, temperature,

carbon dioxide levels) then either medium would do, provided the potato dextrose agar (PDA) was all made as one batch. If nutritional factors were included, only Czapek–Dox medium would be suitable, made up as suggested in (i).

(iii) Either medium would do, provided the PDA was all made with the same potatoes. It would then be dispensed into smaller amounts, each with a different buffer added.

(iv) Only Czapek–Dox medium is suitable, making it with different carbon sources, such as lactose or galactose instead of sucrose.

(v) Either medium would do, provided the PDA was all made with the same potatoes.

Czapek–Dox medium could be used for all the experiments listed, but where PDA can be used it may be preferable to do so as it is less time-consuming to make. On the other hand, Czapek–Dox medium is always the same, which means experiments could be repeated. PDA made on a subsequent occasion would be slightly different, due to variations in potatoes.

2.3 To allow the agar tablets to absorb water and dissolve properly.

2.4 If too much steam builds up, the safety valve may release all the pressure.

2.5 The McCartney bottles are removed from the autoclave, then placed on their sides with their lid end raised slightly. When the agar has solidified, the bottles can be stood upright.

2.6 Agar solidifies at 42 °C. An easy way to test for this is to hold the flask in the palm of the hand. Between 50 °C and 42 °C it can be held comfortably.

2.7 To destroy any microorganisms from the atmosphere which may be present there.

2.8 Flaming the neck of the flask; holding the bung in the hand and replacing it quickly; lifting the petri dish lid only a little, and holding it above the plate while pouring; not putting the petri dish lid down on the bench; working in the vicinity of a bunsen burner.

2.9 If agar is present on the lid, microorganisms will grow on it and obscure the view of the base. If it splashes between the lid and base, it is possible that microorganisms from the petri dish might grow on the agar and escape.

2.10 Plastic items like these would melt at the temperature of an autoclave.

2.11 The optical density is 30%. You could find the number of cells in a stated volume of this sample using a haemocytometer.

2.12 Student **A** used a haemocytometer, which gives a total cell count. Some of the cells this student counted were dead, but dead cells and live cells cannot be distinguished by appearance. Student **B** used pour plates, which involves incubating the cells and counting the colonies which develop. Colonies can only grow from living cells, so this method gives a viable count which will be lower.

2.13 The white bacteria are aerobic and can only grow at the surface where there is plenty of oxygen. The yellow bacteria are facultative anaerobes, and can survive lower oxygen levels. Some oxygen is available to the yellow bacteria because it diffuses down the 'stab' and into the agar gel.

2.14 *Obligate anaerobe*: these are microorganisms which can only grow in the absence of oxygen, such as *Clostridium botulinum*.
Facultative anaerobe: these are microorganisms which grow aerobically when oxygen is present, but can grow (less efficiently) when oxygen is absent, such as *E. coli*.
Mesophile: these are microorganisms which grow best at 20–40 °C, such as *E. coli*.
Psychrophile: these microorganisms grow best at temperatures below 20 °C, such as *Listeria monocytogenes*.

2.15 **a** The carbon source is sucrose.
b The nitrogen sources are ammonium nitrate and potassium nitrate.

2.16 Plant tissue culture may be carried out using plant cells which do not contain chloroplasts, for example, cells from a root. The carbon source is necessary for the plant cells to use in respiration. Even explants which do contain chloroplasts may not be able to photosynthesise enough in the early stages to provide all the energy and organic materials needed by the rapidly growing plant.

2.17 Plant cells, even under optimum conditions, only divide slowly, perhaps once every 24 hours. Microbial cells, on the other hand, multiply rapidly. Therefore, if just one fungal spore or bacterial cell were to contaminate the plant tissue being cultured, the microorganism could outgrow the plant cells in just a few days.

Chapter 3

3.1 This means that air from the laboratory does not directly mix with external air, and vice versa. If a microorganism were to contaminate the air in the laboratory, it would therefore be contained within the laboratory, and the spillage could be dealt with. It also avoids contaminating microorganisms in the external environment from entering easily.

3.2 Bacteriophages readily infect their host bacteria and replicate rapidly, so any bacteriophage infection would quickly destroy the bacterial cells in an industrial fermenter.

3.3 **a** The footbath reduces the number of contaminating microorganisms being brought into the room on the soles of shoes. Since the fermenters have open tops, it would be possible for these organisms to enter the fermenters unless hygiene precautions are taken.
b Fruit naturally contains yeasts, so the fruit is sterilised. Sterile air is pumped into the drums to remove the fruit so that there is no risk of microorganisms in the air contaminating it.
c Ultraviolet light destroys bacteria and fungal spores so keeping the area more hygienic.

3.4 Any three of: an air lock at the entrance; laminar flow cabinet; smooth and easy-to-clean work surfaces, walls and floors; filtered air; designated 'clean zone'.

3.5 **a** The stirrer stirs contents of fermenter so that cells are constantly brought in contact with fresh medium.
b The water jacket contains cold water which circulates constantly to keep contents of fermenter from overheating.
c The acid/alkali inlet introduces acid or alkali as necessary to keep the pH constant.
d The sterile air inlet allows sterile air into the fermenter to provide oxygen for the cells if fermentation is aerobic. If the fermentation is anaerobic, carbon dioxide or nitrogen may be added, since a gas helps to mix the contents of the fermenter.
e The air outlet allows the waste gases and any sterile gas which has been introduced through the air inlet to escape from the fermenter.

3.6 The growth curve for continuous culture will resemble a normal batch culture curve except that, once the culture enters the logarithmic/ exponential growth phase, the cell numbers are kept constant by removing cells and products and adding fresh nutrients at a carefully controlled rate (see figure).

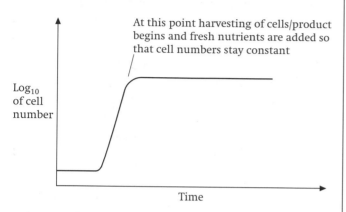

● **Answer for** SAQ 3.6

The number of microorganisms present is kept constant because microorganisms are removed from the fermenter at the same rate as they are formed.

3.7　**a** To ensure purity of the source organism and to ensure antibiotic is being produced.

　　b Temperature, pH, oxygen levels, nutrients.

　　c *Temperature*: temperature probe plus cold water jacket to cool the fermenter.

　　　　pH: pH probe, pH adjusted by addition of buffer, acid or alkali.

　　　　Oxygen content: measured by oxygen probe. This would lead to adjustment of oxygen flow rate and mechanical stirring.

　　　　Nutrients: sometimes additional nutrients are added during the fermentation.

d The fermenter and medium would probably be steam sterilised. Chemical sterilisation of the fermenter may be carried out, but only in unusual circumstances.

e If some of the microorganisms have mutated, this would lead to the mutant organism being cultured and a changed product might result.

f *Advantages*: increases profit, reduces waste, low levels of antibiotic present would control infections in animals that were fed it. *Disadvantages*: If animals are constantly exposed to low levels of antibiotics, their gut micro-organisms develop antibiotic resistance, which can then be passed on to more harmful microorganisms like *Salmonella*. This means that the animals may develop infections which do not respond to antibiotics.

3.8 This is because the *Fusarium* fungus is growing very rapidly, so there will be a great deal of protein synthesis going on.

3.9　**a** The carbon source for penicillin production is glucose and lactose. The nitrogen source is yeast extract.

　　b The carbon source for mycoprotein is glucose and the nitrogen source is ammonia gas and ammonium phosphate.

3.10 Penicillin uses a batch process because penicillin is a secondary metabolite, produced late in the life-cycle of the fungus. Penicillin production is highest when nutrients are low. Mycoprotein consists of the harvested cells, so greatest yields are obtained by continuous fermentation, which keeps the fungus dividing at its maximum rate.

Chapter 4

4.1

GGCATGAATCTATTAGCGA AGCTTCCCGGGATCTACTGG AATTCGCCGA AGCTTTC
CCGTACTTAGATAATCGCTTCGA AGGGCCCTAGATGACCTTAA GCGGCTTCGA AAG

⋯⋯ = *Hind*III restriction sites

╱ = *Eco*R1 restriction site

4.2 These microorganisms are able to survive at high temperatures, therefore their enzymes must have a high optimum temperature. This means they would be able to operate efficiently at high temperatures in an industrial fermenter. However, they would require the fermenter to be heated at the start of the fermentation.

4.3 Many possible answers could be given, including the ability to fix nitrogen, grow in saline soils, or produce increased yields.

4.4 People are concerned that the organisms might cause diseases or release toxins in humans or animals who accidentally ingest them. They are also concerned that they might mutate and become harmful; that they might compete with naturally present organisms, and that a bacterial insecticide might kill beneficial insects.

4.5 *Advantages*: increased milk yield per cow, therefore reducing costs by allowing the farmer to maintain a smaller herd. It can also help to overcome the seasonal shortfall of milk in August. *Disadvantages*: Prolonged use of BST may weaken cows by depleting the immune system; in the EU there is already a milk surplus; cows need to eat more food when given BST, and this cost can offset the additional milk yield; concern about consumers drinking milk or eating milk containing BST, particularly pregnant or nursing mothers.

4.6 This is to ensure that the strain of bacteria is kept pure, and that contaminating microorganisms which might produce other, harmful, substances do not multiply.

4.7 This is mainly because it keeps costs down. There is little point in using an existing food material since the cost of the single cell protein grown on such a substrate would be much more expensive. People will only use single cell protein as a food source if it is cheaper than existing foodstuffs. Waste products can be expensive for a company to dispose of, but if they can be used to make a saleable product this can make a profit instead.

4.8 Variables include: type of milk used; species of bacteria in the starter culture; amount of pressing to remove whey; length of time the cheese is left to ripen; whether cheese is inoculated with a mould; and the presence of microorganisms on the outer surface of the cheese.

4.9 Milk may become contaminated with antibiotics if a cow has been treated with antibiotics, for example to treat mastitis, and the correct time has not elapsed before using her milk for human consumption. The milk used to make yogurt must be free from antibiotics, since antibiotics would destroy the bacteria used in the starter culture.

4.10 If the milk mixture is too hot, the bacteria in the starter culture will be destroyed.

4.11 This is because the bacteria produce acids, such as lactic acid and methanoic acid.

4.12 The bacteria are not harmful. Indeed, many people feel that 'live' yogurt is healthier and tastes better.

4.13 This sterilisation is necessary to ensure that contaminating microorganisms, such as yeasts, do not enter the yogurt, vats or pipework. This is usually done by steam sterilisation, although chemicals might be used if laboratory tests suggested that contamination had occurred.

4.14 A 'top-fermenting' yeast forms a thick frothy layer on top of the beer, whereas a 'bottom-fermenting' yeast forms a layer at the bottom of the fermenter. 'Top-fermenters' are mainly used for beer, while 'bottom-fermenters' are mainly used for lagers.

4.15 This is because the microorganisms are kept in their exponential growth phase in continuous fermenters. For organisms to be growing exponentially, conditions must be at their optimum, which means that waste products must be kept at lower levels. Alcohol is the waste product of the yeast, and if it accumulates, yeast growth slows down.

4.16 Arguments for: improving palatability of meat; reducing the time needed in cold storage after slaughter, thereby saving costs and giving the meat a longer shelf-life. Main argument against: injection is distressing to the animal and may cause suffering.

4.17 A patent is the exclusive right to manufacture or use an invention. Companies may not always obtain a patent because:
- the invention may not be sufficiently different from other patented inventions so a patent may not be granted;
- in filing a patent, companies must give a detailed description. They may feel this could give their competitors an advantage and so decide to keep the invention a trade secret instead.

4.18 It would be a gene which renders the organism unlikely to survive in a normal environment. For example, it might be a gene for a faulty enzyme so that the organism is unable to synthesise an essential amino acid. In the laboratory, this amino acid can be supplied in the medium, but in the external environment, the amino acid is unlikely to be found.

Chapter 5

5.1 **a** Unfused lymphocytes die because they cannot divide in culture.

b Lymphocytes need to be fused with myeloma cells because they are cancer cells, which divide rapidly and easily.

5.2 If the woman is not pregnant, HCG will not bind to the antibody on the dipstick because there is no HCG in her urine. This means that the second antibody will not attach to the 'dipstick'. As the second antibody is attached to the enzyme, the chemical dye will not change colour.

5.3 **a** The amino acid sequence of factor VIII is converted to triplet codes.

b A length of DNA is synthesised which codes for factor VIII.

c A plasmid is cut with a restriction enzyme and the gene for factor VIII is inserted.

d The plasmid is inserted into a bacterium.

e The bacterium is grown in a fermenter in large numbers

f Factor VIII is produced by the bacterium and extracted from the fermenter.

5.4 The gene coding for the antigen will be introduced into a banana cell culture using a suitable vector. One method might be to use *Agrobacterium tumefaciens* as shown on page 55.

5.5 The biosensor would contain the enzyme glucose oxidase immobilised on the surface of the probe. In the presence of glucose in the blood, the enzyme would produce gluconic acid. This would generate a positive charge on the surface of the probe, causing a flow of electrons to the transducer, proportional to the glucose concentration in the blood. The current can be used to operate a pump which releases insulin into the bloodstream, and lowers the blood glucose level. The reduced blood glucose level would result in a lower current being received by the transducer, so the pump would slow down.

5.6 The probe of the biosensor could have an enzyme immobilised on its surface which breaks down cholesterol or alcohol to organic acids. The resulting drop in pH level would be detected by the transducer as a flow of electrons, and this current could be read on a meter. The current would be proportional to the amount of cholesterol or alcohol in the blood.

Chapter 6

6.1 A variety of other enzymes would have been present, including lipases and amylases.

6.2 The substrates mentioned are mainly carbohydrate-based. Whey contains a watery solution of lactose, molasses contains sucrose and starch, and flour waste is mainly starch.

6.3 Any suitable suggestion is acceptable, provided it is cheap, plentiful and non-toxic. One example might be water which has been used to wash potato slices prior to frozen chip or potato crisp manufacture.

6.4 The liquor has a higher water potential than the solution, so water passes by osmosis from the liquor to the solution across the membrane, down a water potential gradient.

6.5 **a** You could use the Biuret test. This tests for proteins, and enzymes are proteins. If the maltose is free of enzymes, the Biuret test will be negative.

b Variables could include: size of beads; enzyme concentration in the bead; length of the column; flow rate of starch through the column; concentration of starch suspension; temperature.

6.6 Many suggestions are possible, but anything which could kill microorganisms is particularly toxic. Some industrial processes produce phenolic compounds or bleaches, for example, which are very harmful to microorganisms.

6.7 This is because the effluent is so rich in organic matter that both treatments are necessary to treat it. Experience has shown that some chemical wastes break down better in the activated sludge process, and others in the trickling filters.

6.8 The fermenter should include a container for the substrate to be placed inside: this might be a pit in the ground or some kind of storage vessel. It should incorporate a cover and a pipe for drawing off the biogas. Some provision would need to be made for adding more waste from time to time. The fermenter would need to be out-of-doors and not too close to houses for safety reasons as methane can be explosive.

6.9 This residue can be used as fertiliser.

Glossary

aerobe An organism which needs molecular oxygen for its metabolism.

agar A jelly-like substance obtained from seaweed (red algae) used to help solidify nutrient media for growing microorganisms.

akinete A vegetative cell which is transformed into a thick-walled, resistant spore in Cyanobacteria.

anaerobe An organism which cannot grow if molecular oxygen is present; strict anaerobes are killed by oxygen, facultative anaerobes will grow if oxygen is present but can also grow if oxygen is absent.

antibiotic A chemical produced by microorganisms, such as bacteria and moulds that, in dilute solution, can kill or inhibit the growth of other microorganisms.

antibody A protein produced by the B lymphocytes of the immune system. Antibodies are very specific and help defend the body against pathogens and foreign molecules by binding to antigens and bringing about their destruction.

antigen A molecule that is recognised and bound by a specific antibody.

ascospore Found only in the ascomycete fungi, these spores are haploid and produced inside a diploid cell called an ascus. There are usually eight ascospores in an ascus since meiosis is followed by mitosis.

aseptic technique A procedure used in microbiology to prevent contamination of cultures by microorganisms from the environment and contamination of the environment by the microorganisms being handled.

autoclave A large pressure cooker used to steam-sterilise laboratory media, glassware and metal instruments under conditions of high temperature and pressure, usually 121 °C at 103 kPa for 20 min.

autolysis Self-digestion of a cell or organism brought about by lysosomes, cell organelles that release the enzyme lysozyme.

autotroph An organism that is able to synthesise the organic materials it requires from inorganic substances in its environment.

B lymphocyte Blood cell responsible for the immune response. When sensitised by an antigen, it differentiates into clones of antibody-producing plasma cells and memory cells.

basidiospore Found only in Basidiomycete fungi, basidiospores are produced by meiosis of a diploid cell, the basidium.

batch culture A culture in which all the ingredients are added at the beginning: it is then left for the reaction to take place, after which the products are harvested.

binary fission The process in which a single-celled organism divides into two daughter cells.

biodegradation The use of microorganisms to break down substances used e.g. in waste treatment and in recycling.

biogas A mixture of methane and carbon dioxide along with traces of other gases, such as hydrogen sulphide, hydrogen and water vapour, that is produced during the anaerobic digestion of organic material by microorganisms.

biomass In microbiology, biomass is the cell mass produced during fermentation. In renewable energy systems, biomass is plant material produced in photosynthesis and animal wastes (e.g. manure).

biosensor An artificial biological sensory system. Biological chemicals (enzymes or antibodies) may be coupled with microelectronics to enable rapid, accurate detection of substances, such as chemicals in body fluids, or pollutants in water.

biotechnology The application of living organisms, or substances made by them, to make products of value to humans.

callus Undifferentiated plant tissue which usually develops as a result of a wound in a plant, but also refers to a mass of undifferentiated plant cells used in plant tissue culture.

capsid The protein coat of a virus.

cell culture Growing cells or tissues in a laboratory, or on an appropriate nutrient medium.

chemoautotroph An organism which uses carbon dioxide as its sole source of carbon and inorganic chemicals as its source of energy.

chitin A tough resistant polysaccharide which is a component of some fungal cell walls.

cilium (plural **cilia**) A short hair-like structure present on the surface of some specialised eukaryotic cells. They are usually arranged in rows and quite numerous. They are used in locomotion in some protoctista, or to cause liquids to flow in a certain direction.

clone A group of genetically identical organisms or cells which are all descended asexually from the same individual.

coccus (plural **cocci**) A sphere-shaped bacterium.

conidium A fungal spore produced by mitosis at the tip of a specialised hypha called a conidiophore.

conjugation In bacteria, the transfer of genetic material from one cell to another by cell to cell contact; pili may be involved. In ciliated protoctistans such as *Paramecium*, the process of exchange of nuclei before replication.

continuous culture A technique used to maintain a culture of bacteria or cells in their rapid growth phase. This is achieved by supplying the fermenter with a continuous supply of nutrients at a balanced rate, while products are continually removed.

dilution plating A technique used to obtain a viable count of bacteria. A bacterial suspension is diluted in a tenfold series, giving dilutions of 10^{-1}, 10^{-2}, 10^{-3} etc. 1 cm^3 of each sample is then plated on to a sterile agar plate and incubated. Each colony that develops has arisen from a single bacterial cell, so the result may be used to calculate the density of live bacterial cells in the original sample.

enzyme immobilisation A technique used to attach an enzyme to a support medium, such as alginate or a matrix of collagen fibres. Immobilised enzymes may be used over and over again without contaminating the product, and immobilisation protects the enzymes to a certain extent from pH and temperature changes.

eukaryotic Cells containing a true nucleus, with a nuclear membrane and membrane-bound organelles.

explant A piece of plant tissue which is used to initiate a plant cell or plant tissue culture.

exponential growth Growth where cell numbers increase logarithmically with time.

feedstock chemicals Chemicals used in large quantities as the starting point for the manufacture of other chemicals.

fermentation The extraction of energy from organic products without the involvement of oxygen. *Or* The use of microorganisms or enzymes extracted from microorganisms to carry out a wide variety of chemical reactions, which may or may not be anaerobic.

flagellum (plural **flagella**) A fine, long, whip-like organelle which protrudes from the cell surface. Used in locomotion and feeding they are common in some protoctista where they have a 9+2 arrangement of microtubules in cross section. They are also found as thread-like organelles on some bacteria, also used in locomotion, they have a much simpler structure in prokaryotes, being a rigid hollow cylinder of protein with a rotating base which propels the cell along.

floc A clumping together of organic particles in a matrix of sticky polysaccharide. This process of flocculation is important in sewage treatment where it helps organic material to settle out.

fungi A kingdom of eukaryotic, mainly multicellular organisms which lack chlorophyll.

gasohol A mixture of petrol and ethanol used to power motor vehicles.

gene A length of DNA which codes for the production of a particular protein.

genetic engineering The application of methods using recombinant DNA to give new genetic traits to an organism by introducing new genes into its cells.

genome The complete set of genes present in an organism.

haemocytometer An apparatus for counting cells, consisting of a grid of known dimensions etched on a glass slide that contains a known volume of liquid.

heterocyst A large, transparent, thick-walled cell found in the filaments of certain Cyanobacteria such as *Anabaena*. They are concerned with nitrogen fixation.

heterotroph An organism which requires organic compounds as its carbon and energy source.

HIV Human Immunodeficiency Virus, shown to be responsible for AIDS (Acquired Immunodeficiency Syndrome)

hybridoma A hybrid cell made by fusing an antibody-producing B-lymphocyte with a myeloma cell. Hybridomas are the source of monoclonal antibodies.

hypha (plural **hyphae**) The single tubular filament of a fungus. Hyphae bundled together form the mycelium.

immunisation A process rendering a host immunity to a disease.

in vitro Latin for 'in glass'. This term refers to biological processes carried out outside a living organism, for example, in a test tube.

inoculation The transfer of microorganisms from one source to another, e.g. transferring bacteria from a broth culture on to a sterile agar plate, or from a starter culture into a fermenter containing sterile medium.

interferons A group of proteins which are active in the immune system. They fight viral infections and stimulate the cell-killing abilities of some immune cells. They are being tested for use in cancer therapy and in the treatment of AIDS and other viral diseases.

interleukins A group of proteins which are required for a normal immune response by initiating the growth and development of immune cells.

kinin A plant growth substance which promotes cell division.

log, logarithm The logarithm of a number is the exponent of that number e.g. $100 = 10^2$. Therefore its $\log_{10} = 2$

lymphocyte A type of white blood cell (agranulocyte) for example B and T cells.

lysis A process of cell destruction often brought about by the enzyme lysozyme.

lytic cycle A virus infection that results in cell lysis.

meristem culture Plant cells cultured from the undifferentiated meristematic tissue from which new cells arise.

mesophile An organism which has an optimum growth between 20 °C and 40 °C, including most human pathogens.

micropropagation The propagation of plants using plant tissue culture techniques.

microtubules Narrow (25 nm diameter) long tubules which are found in the cytoplasm of many eukaryotic cells and in flagella.

monoclonal antibody An antibody produced by a clone of hybridoma cells. Monoclonal antibody technology allows large quantities of pure antibody to be produced.

murein A peptidoglycan which is a cell wall component of prokaryotes.

mycelium Composed of a mass of fungal hyphae tangled together.

myeloma A tumour of the B lymphocytes which normally produce antibodies. Myeloma cells are fused with selected cells to make hybridomas for the production of monoclonal antibodies.

nutrient agar plates These are sterile petri dishes filled with sterile nutrient agar, ready for bacteria to grow on. The nutrient agar contains nutrients for the bacteria to grow on, such as peptone, meat extract and sodium chloride together with agar as a setting agent.

nutrient broth A liquid medium containing nutrients for bacteria to grow in. It contains the same nutrients as nutrient agar but does not have a setting agent.

pathogen A microorganism or virus that causes disease.

peptidoglycan A macromolecule composed of amino acid and sugar units. It forms the basis of prokaryotic cell walls. One example is murein.

phagocytosis The process by which certain types of cell engulf solid material and destroy it using digestive enzymes.

plant tissue culture A technique used for the growth of plant cells *in vitro*. There are several different methods, but they all use a sterile plant growth medium such as Murashige and Skoog medium. The technique is useful for rapid propagation of commercially important plants.

plasmid A small, usually circular molecule of DNA that occurs in bacteria but is not part of the bacterial chromosome. Plasmids have been used as cloning vectors to transfer genes between species.

Prokaryotae A kingdom of microscopic, mainly unicellular microorganisms, including bacteria. Their DNA is circular, naked, and not situated inside a nuclear membrane. Prokaryotic cells also lack membrane-bound organelles, such as mitochondria.

Protoctista A kingdom of microscopic, eukaryotic organisms. They may be unicellular or multicellular, and mainly show sexual reproduction. It is a diverse group including heterotrophic and photosynthetic organisms.

protoplasts Plant cells that have had their rigid cellulose cell walls removed. They are fused to produce cell hybrids and used as targets for gene transfer in plant genetic engineering.

R-plasmid (R-factor) A circle of DNA found in some bacteria which confers resistance to antibiotics or antibodies.

recombinant DNA A DNA molecule that has been formed by joining together segments of DNA from two or more sources.

recombinant protein A protein made by genetic engineering, usually in bacteria, yeast or cultured cells, as the product of a gene that has been inserted into a recombinant DNA molecule.

restriction enzyme A bacterial enzyme that cuts DNA at a specific sequence of nucleotides and is used for making recombinant DNA.

reverse osmosis A process used to remove excess water during an industrial process. An artificial diffusion gradient is set up across a selectively permeable membrane, which draws water across.

reverse transcriptase Enzymes which synthesise DNA from an RNA template. In genetic engineering, these are used to manufacture complementary DNA from messenger RNA.

risk assessments A risk assessment must be carried out before starting any microbiological work. It involves considering any potential hazards in the work, so that steps may be taken to minimise any risk to health or safety.

secondary metabolism This usually occurs at some specific point in an organism's life cycle, when a change is taking place, such as aging or spore formation. Antibiotics are examples of secondary metabolites.

sporangiophore A stalk-like structure in fungi, with a sporangium at the tip.

sporangium (plural **sporangia**) A specialised structure in fungi in which spores are produced.

sticky ends Unpaired nucleotides at the end of a DNA double helix. They may be produced by using restriction enzymes to cut DNA at certain base sequences during genetic engineering. They can be made to fuse with complementary DNA sequences from another source, using ligase enzymes.

substrate A compound acted on by an enzyme and converted to a product.

thermophile An organism with an optimum temperature for growth above $40\,^{\circ}C$. Thermophiles are adapted for growth in hot temperatures such as volcanic springs.

total cell count This is a measure of all the cells, whether living or dead, in a known volume of a culture of microorganisms. One method for determining the total cell count involves using a haemocytometer.

turbidimetry This is a method of estimating the numbers of cells in a culture by determining optical density (cloudiness). A spectrophotometer is used to shine light through a culture. The more cells present in the culture, the less light will pass through.

vector In biotechnology, a vector is a DNA molecule which is used to transfer genes into cells; usually this is plasmid or viral DNA.

viable Live; capable of reproducing.

viruses A particle containing a nucleic acid core, either DNA or RNA, surrounded by a protein coat called a capsid. Viruses are obligate parasites that reproduce by entering cells and taking over the cell's own protein synthesising mechanisms.

Index